FACTS AT YOUR FINGERTIPS

FISH

BROWN
BEAR
BOOKS

Published by Brown Bear Books Limited

An imprint of
The Brown Reference Group plc
68 Topstone Road
Redding
Connecticut
06896
USA
www.brownreference.com

© 2006 The Brown Reference Group plc

Library of Congress Cataloging-in-Publication Data available upon request.

ISBN-10: 1-933834-01-3
ISBN-13: 978-1-93383-401-6

Authors: John Dawes with Amy-Jane Beer and David Alderton

Editorial Director: Lindsey Lowe

Project Director: Graham Bateman

Art Director: Steve McCurdy

Editor: Derek Hall, Virginia Carter

Artists: Mick Loates with Denys Ovenden and Colin Newman

Printed in China

Jacket artwork: Front: Denys Ovenden (Top); Colin Newman (Center, Bottom).
Reverse: Mick Loates.

Contents

3

Introduction

Fish are masters of our oceans, rivers, and lakes and are the most conspicuous fauna of these habitats. Many species are also vitally important as food for people around the world. The first fishlike animals known from fossils date back some 480 million years to the Ordovician Period. The earliest fish were jawless, a feature still retained today in hagfish and lampreys. Fish with true jaws (known as acanthodians) did not evolve for another 40–50 million years. It is from such fish that modern-day fish have arisen, although many have gone extinct along the way, including the acanthodians themselves.

Today there are over 26,700 species of fish. They range in size from the tiny dwarf pygmy goby (*Pandaka pygmaea*) from Asia, which grows to only 0.4 inches (9 mm), to the globally distributed giant whale shark (*Rhinocodon typus*), which can reach 59 feet (18 m).

What Makes a Fish?

Strangely no single feature seems to be totally unique to fish (for example, some amphibians have gills, and many reptiles have scales). Rather it is a combination of features that defines a fish, and most species have all or most of the following characteristics:

- A braincase and limb (fin) skeleton consisting of cartilage or bone.
- Fins, usually (but not always) with spines or supporting rays.
- Breathe through outward directed gills covered by a gill cover (operculum), which results in an external slitlike aperture or a series of slits.
- Bodies usually (but not always) covered in scales.
- A swim bladder used in buoyancy (exceptions include sharks).
- A sensory organ known as the lateral line running in a head to tail direction or another series of sensory pits (as in sharks).
- Cold blooded (poikilothermic)—in other words, the body temperature matches that of the environment (some fish such as tuna can raise their temperature above that of the surrounding water).

Rank	Scientific name	Common name
Phylum	Chordata	Animals with a backbone
Superclass	Gnathostomata	Jawed fish
Class	Actinopterygii	Ray-finned fish
Order	Characiformes	Characoids
Family	Characidae	Characins
Genus	*Pygocentrus*	Piranhas
Species	*natereri*	Red-bellied piranha

The kingdom Animalia is subdivided into groups such as classes, families, genera, and species. Above is the classification of the red-bellied piranha.

Fish are adaptable creatures that are found virtually everywhere there is water. The habitats they occupy include the Arctic wastes, fast-flowing mountain streams, slow-flowing rivers, tiny mud pools no larger than an elephant's footprint, crystal-clear warm water reefs, the open sea, the dark cold abysses of the world's oceans where no light reaches, and the water that flows through cave systems.

Naming Fish

Just by looking, we can see that piranhas and perches are probably related, since they look alike, and that eels are quite different from sharks. Scientists take this study much further in the science of taxonomy, in which detailed relationships are worked out using a hierarchy of categories called taxa. The classification (arrangement) of the taxa of fish is particularly complicated. There is much debate among scientists about the classification of fish, and changes occur frequently. The system used here is based on that of Joseph S. Nelson (*Fishes of the World*, John Wiley and Sons, Inc., 1994) with some modifications.

Fish are divided into two broad groups. First, there are the jawless fish in the superclass Agnatha, which contains just 90 or so species in two distinct types—lampreys and hagfish. Second, there are the jawed fish in the superclass Gnathostomata, which contains the remaining species. Jawed fish are subdivided into cartilaginous fish and bony fish. The cartilaginous fish include the sharks and the rays and form the grade Chondrichthiomorphi, with a single class—Chondrichthyes. The bony fish such as eels, piranhas, and perches make up the grade Teleostomi. Beneath these broad categories fish are further divided into other groups (classes, subclasses, divisions, subdivisions, superorders, etc.). The major taxonomic groups with which the lay reader probably identifies are the orders, of which there are about 58. For example, all catfish belong to the order Siluriformes. In this book you will find representatives of many fish orders. They are grouped together under headings related to various higher taxa, and are color coded.

Within an order such as Characiformes, all piranhalike fish are placed in the family Characidae along with, for example, tetras. Very closely related piranhas are mostly placed in the genus *Pygocentrus*. Finally, individual piranha species, for example, the red-bellied piranha and the San Francisco piranha, are distinguished by the scientific names *Pygocentrus natteri* and *Pygocentrus piraya* respectively. A classification for the red piranha is shown on opposite page.

About this Book

In *Facts at Your Fingertips: Fish* you will find illustrated entries on 112 species of fish or groups of related fish. Each entry follows a fixed structure. The color-coded header strip denotes the group to which each fish belongs, followed by its common name. The fact panel then gives the scientific name of the fish (or group) in question and other taxonomic information. The next section describes different features of the fish and

their lifestyles. The artwork illustrates either the species that is the subject of the entry or, if the entry discusses a group of fish, a representative species. In the latter case a brief caption is also given, often including the size of the species.

The first two entries (Sea Squirts and Salps, Lancelets) deal with groups that, while not fish, are the earliest forms of existing life that share some characteristics with chordates (the major group that includes fish as well as reptiles, amphibians, birds, and mammals).

The survival of many fish, like all animals, is in doubt as they endure and suffer from the pressures brought on them by people. Under the heading "Status," information is given on the threats facing these fish, if any. For definitions of the categories of threat see Glossary under IUCN and CITES.

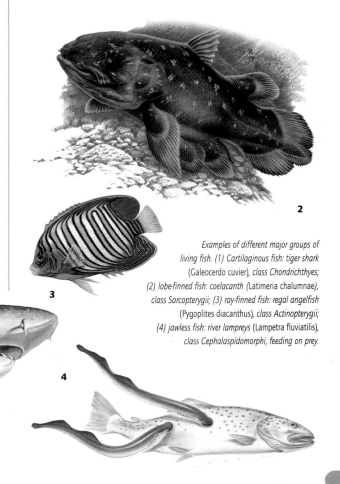

Examples of different major groups of living fish. (1) Cartilaginous fish: tiger shark (Galeocerdo cuvier), class Chondrichthyes; (2) lobe-finned fish: coelacanth (Latimeria chalumnae), class Sarcopterygii; (3) ray-finned fish: regal angelfish (Pygoplites diacanthus), class Actinopterygii; (4) jawless fish: river lampreys (Lampetra fluviatilis), class Cephalaspidomorphi, feeding on prey.

Sea Squirts and Salps

The 6-inch (15-cm) sea vase (*Ciona intestinalis*) is common in docks, harbors, and estuaries in shallow northeast Atlantic waters.

Common name Sea squirts and salps

Classes Ascidiacea (sea squirts), Thaliacea (salps), Larvacea (larvaceans)

Subphylum Urochordata (Tunicata)

Number of species Ascidiacea: about 1,850; Thaliacea: about 70; Larvacea: about 70

Size Individuals from 0.04 in (1 mm) to about 8 in (20 cm) long; colonies up to 40 in (1 m) in sea squirts and over 10 ft (3 m) in salps

Key features Adult sea squirts sedentary, solitary, or colonial; often flask-shaped, sheathed in test or tunic, with gills in hollow center (atrium); no head; inhalant siphon at top of body to take in sea water, exhalant siphon on side to expel water; larval sea squirts tadpolelike, free swimming, and quite different from adults, with chordate characteristics: gill slits, tail behind anus, hollow dorsal nerve cord, and notochord—the forerunner of a backbone; all these features lost on metamorphosis to adult form; in salps both larvae and adults free swimming; adults form colonies in a variety of shapes, e.g., like casks or chains; adult larvaceans solitary, free swimming, and retain some larval characteristics

Breeding Adults hermaphrodite; asexual reproduction involves budding new adults from parent; in sexual reproduction eggs and sperm released into atrium or into open water for fertilization

Diet Food particles filtered from sea water

Habitat Adult Ascidiacea attached to rocks and other organisms on seabed; Thaliacea and Larvacea found in open water

Distribution Worldwide; mostly in shallow oceans and seas, but with some species to 650 ft (200 m)

Status Not threatened

Lancelets

The 4-inch (10-cm) lancelet (*Branchiostoma lanceolatum*) lives in shallow inshore waters in both tropical and temperate regions.

Common name Lancelets

Order Amphioxiformes

Subphylum Cephalochordata (Acrania)

Number of species About 25 in 2 genera: *Branchiostoma* (or *Amphioxus*) and *Epigonichthys*

Size Up to 4 in (10 cm)

Key features Simple, fishlike chordates lacking recognizable head but with hood of tentacles in *Branchiostoma*; have hollow dorsal nerve cord similar to vertebrates, but with notochord instead of vertebrae; body slender and pointed at both ends; distinct muscle blocks in segments; gills well developed; dorsal fin extends from just behind the head to the well-formed tail; a small ventral fin extends from the atriopore to the anus

Breeding Sexes separate; eggs and sperm released into open water where fertilization takes place; free-swimming planktonic tornaria larvae

Diet Filter feeder; water is channeled into the mouth cavity by ring of tentacles around the mouth and then filtered through gill slits in the pharynx (throat); particles are mixed with mucus and move to the intestine to be digested; excess water flows into an area surrounding the pharynx and is discharged through the atriopore

Habitat Inshore shallow water

Distribution Temperate and tropical seas

Status Not threatened

Hagfish and Lampreys

A 24-inch (61-cm) hagfish (*Myxine* species), showing its elongated, eel-like form, simple fin, and mouth tentacles.

Common name Hagfish and lampreys

Classes Myxini (comprising hagfish: order Myxiniformes, family Myxinidae); Cephalaspidomorphi (comprising lampreys: order Petromyzontiformes, family Petromyzontidae)

Superclass Agnatha

Subphylum Vertebrata (Craniata)

Size Up to 46 in (1.2 m) in hagfish; up to 36 in (90 cm) in lampreys

Number of species Hagfish: about 50 in 6 genera; lampreys: about 40 in 7 genera

Key features Lampreys: eel-like with 1 or 2 dorsal fins and simple caudal fin; no biting jaws; mouth a disk with horny teeth; 7 gill openings; ammocete larval stage very different from adult; hagfish: eel-like, white to pale brown, with fleshy median fin and 4-6 tentacles around mouth; no biting jaws

Breeding Lampreys: spawn in rivers and streams, freshwater species moving upstream and marine species entering from sea; some with complex life cycles; hagfish: lay a few large eggs at sea

Diet Lampreys: as larvae, particles filtered from water; parasitic adults attach to host fish and feed on blood and tissues; nonparasitic adults do not feed; hagfish: dead or dying fish and sea mammals on seafloor

Habitat Lampreys: seas and rivers; hagfish: seabed

Distribution Lampreys: temperate marine and freshwater; hagfish: mostly temperate oceans and seas (excluding midocean zones) but also cooler, deeper tropical waters

Status Not threatened

Elephant Fish

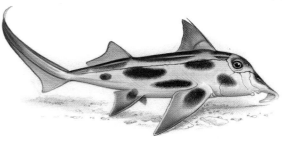

Common name Elephant fish (southern beauty, ghost shark)

Scientific name *Callorhynchus milii*

Family Callorhynchidae

Order Chimaeriformes

Size 4 ft (1.2 m)

Key features Two tall triangular dorsal fins present along the back, with a sharp, venomous spine in front of the first dorsal fin; upper lobe of caudal fin is triangular and rather sharklike; very evident protuberance in front of mouth; basic coloration silvery with variable brown markings over body; lives in deep water, coming closer inshore when breeding

Breeding Egg laying; breeds seasonally; eggs relatively large—about 4 in (10 cm) wide and 10 in (25 cm) long; yellowish brown in color; deposited on sandy seabed; young develop slowly in egg cases and begin to hatch from May onward after an interval of 6-8 months; newborn young measure about 4 in (10 cm) long and develop slowly

Diet Invertebrates, mainly different types of shellfish

Habitat Continental shelf; relatively deep water down to 660 ft (200 m); in southern spring they move into shallower areas and are not found below 130 ft (40 m)

Distribution Southern Pacific Ocean around New Zealand, breeding mainly along eastern coast of South Island; sometimes caught off North Island; also encountered off coast of Australia, becoming more common moving south from New South Wales down to Tasmania and South Australia

Status Highly vulnerable because of overfishing

Whale Shark

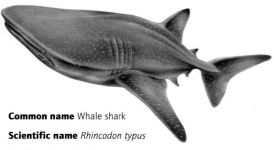

Common name Whale shark

Scientific name *Rhincodon typus*

Family Rhincodontidae

Order Orectolobiformes

Size Around 39 ft (12 m), but may grow to 59 ft (18 m)

Key features Whalelike body with massive, flat head; truncated snout; cavernous mouth with numerous small teeth; body base color grayish with light spots and stripes—the pattern unique to each individual; underside white; 3 distinct ridges along top of body

Breeding Little information available; females may retain fertilized eggs within their bodies until they hatch; up to 300 developing embryos may be held at different stages of development by a single female; newborn whale sharks thought to measure only up to 28 in (71 cm)

Diet Zooplankton, small fish, and other small animals filtered out in vast volumes by the gill rakers

Habitat Both inshore and oceanic waters; found from the surface down to a depth of around 425 ft (130 m)

Distribution Tropical and temperate waters in the Atlantic, Indian, and Pacific Oceans.

Status Listed by IUCN as Vulnerable; legally protected in the Philippines since 1998; the species is particularly vulnerable to exploitation due to its slow rate of reproduction and growth, its highly migratory nature, and low abundance; in recent years dive tourism has developed in a number of locations around the world

Tasseled Wobbegong

Common name Tasseled wobbegong

Scientific name *Eucrossorhinus dasypogon*

Family Orectolobidae

Order Orectolobiformes

Size Maximum size usually around 4 ft (1.2 m); occasionally reported up to 12 ft (3.7 m)

Key features Flattened body and large, flattened head; numerous ornate skin flaps around the mouth; large mouth located at front of head—not underslung as in most other sharks; body covered in irregular mottled patterns that provide excellent camouflage; fanglike teeth; 2 dorsal fins, approximately equal in size; large pectoral and pelvic fins

Breeding Mating season and duration of pregnancy unknown; number of offspring unknown; embryos obtain nourishment from their yolk sacs during development; may be around 8 in (20 cm) long at birth

Diet Feeds close to the bottom on fish and invertebrates; lies motionless in wait for prey during daylight hours and gulps in any suitable victim that swims within range; during hours of darkness becomes more mobile and actively hunts prey, including crabs, lobsters, squid, octopuses, and fish (even other sharks)

Habitat Shallow, inland waters down to around 130 ft (40 m)

Distribution Western Pacific Ocean, Northern Australia (from Queensland to Western Australia), Indonesia, Papua New Guinea, and Irian Jaya

Status Listed by IUCN as Near Threatened due to coral-reef habitat destruction

Dogfish

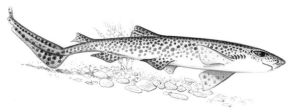

Common name Dogfish (rough hound, lesser-spotted cat shark)

Scientific name *Scyliorhinus canicula*

Family Scyliorhinidae

Order Carcharhiniformes

Size Up to around 3.9 ft (1.2 m), although usually smaller

Key features Slim body and slightly flattened head; body generally light-colored and liberally peppered with dark brown spots; some specimens exhibit lighter spots or dark blotches; large dark eyes; underslung mouth; well-formed pectoral fins, but all other fins—including caudal—relatively small

Breeding During winter months large numbers of females gather close to shore and are joined by males as spring approaches; mating usually occurs later in summer in deeper water, with males entwining their slender bodies around their mates; internal fertilization; females return to shallower water to lay eggs; 18–20 egg cases laid, two at a time; tendrils of egg cases wrap around seaweeds, corals, or any submerged object; incubation 9 months

Diet Mainly bottom-dwelling mollusks (including whelks and clams) and crustaceans (predominantly shrimp and crabs); also bony fish such as seahorses and flatfish, as well as soft-bodied invertebrates like worms and sea cucumbers

Habitat Bottom dwelling; reported at a depth of over 1,300 ft (396 m), but usually at a maximum depth of around 330 ft (100 m), with preferred habitat considerably shallower, including intertidal zone

Distribution Eastern Atlantic from Norway south to the Canary Islands; also Mediterranean

Status Not threatened

Gray Reef Shark

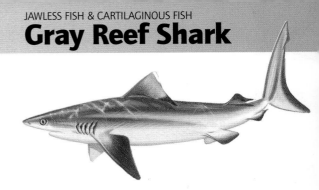

Common name Gray reef shark (long-nosed blacktail shark)

Scientific name *Carcharhinus amblyrhynchos*

Family Carcharhinidae

Order Carcharhiniformes

Size Up to 8.4 ft (2.6 m) but usually smaller

Key features Sleek, dark-gray or bronze-gray back fading to white on the underside; long snout with underslung mouth; caudal fin has distinct black edge (hence one of the shark's common names); some individuals have white-tipped first dorsal fin (they are regarded as *C. wheeleri* by some authorities)

Breeding Internal fertilization; embryos develop a placenta through which they obtain nourishment for up to 1 year; 1–6 pups produced in a litter

Diet Wide range of bony fish, as well as squid, octopuses, lobsters, and crabs

Habitat On continental and island shelves and on coral reefs, preferring deeper waters around the dropoff zone (where the reef plunges sharply at its ocean-facing edge); also found in atoll passes and in shallower areas with strong currents; during the day groups of individuals may rest on the bottom—unlike most sharks, they do not need to swim continuously to force oxygen-rich water to flow over their gills

Distribution Widely distributed in tropical zones of both the Pacific and Indian Oceans; if *C. wheeleri* is accepted as being a variant of *C. amblyrhynchos*, rather than a separate species, then the range extends into the Red Sea and down as far as South Africa

Status Listed by IUCN as Lower Risk near threatened; abundant at many locations within its range, but may be declining in some areas due to fishing; considered of value if protected for dive tourism

Tiger Shark

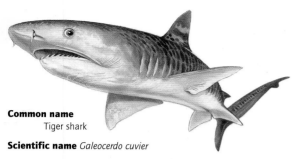

Common name
Tiger shark

Scientific name *Galeocerdo cuvier*

Family Carcharhinidae

Order Carcharhiniformes

Size Commonly attains a length of 10-14 ft (3-4.3 m) and weighs between 850-1,400 lb (385-635 kg); maximum length reported 24.3 ft (7.4 m) and a weight of over 6,855 lb (3,110 kg)

Key features Snout broad and blunt; large mouth with large serrated (cock's comb) teeth; grayish body with darker vertical bars forming "tiger" pattern; patterning particularly well pronounced in juveniles, but fading with age; white underside; top lobe of caudal fin long and powerful

Breeding Livebearing species in which litter sizes vary between 11 and 82 pups; gestation up to 12-13 months; newborn pups measure 20-40 in (51-102 cm)

Diet Extremely varied—virtually anything edible; also swallows an array of nonedible items, including bottles, cans, pieces of metal, rubber tires, money, cloth, sacks of coal, and even explosives; species sometimes described as the ocean's "dustbin with fins"; attacks and saws chunks off prey from very first bite (instead of biting and then releasing), not allowing victim a chance to escape; consequently responsible for more human fatalities than the great white shark

Habitat From intertidal zone down to depths of around 460 ft (140 m); reported as being able to descend to around 1,000 ft (305 m) or deeper; usually found near the surface and frequently in river estuaries and lagoons; may be found in the open ocean but is not a true oceanic species

Distribution Widely distributed in most tropical and warm-temperate regions, but not found in the Mediterranean

Status Listed by IUCN as Lower Risk near threatened due to declines of several populations where heavily fished

Hammerheads

The great hammerhead (*Sphyrna mokarran*) has been known to attack humans.
Length to 20 feet (6.1 m).

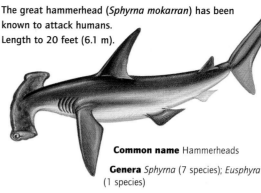

Common name Hammerheads

Genera *Sphyrna* (7 species); *Eusphyra* (1 species)

Family Carcharhinidae (sometimes placed in their own family, Sphyrnidae)

Order Carcharhiniformes

Size Smallest: scalloped hammerhead (*S. lewini*)—3 feet (90 cm); largest: great hammerhead (*S. mokarran*)—around 19.7 ft (6 m)

Key features Characteristic and variable lateral lobes on head (the "hammer"); eyes at ends of "hammer"; nostrils widely spaced near outer front extremities of "hammer"; body powerfully muscled; first dorsal fin high and prominent, second very small; pectoral fins small; caudal fin with long, pointed upper lobe bearing a distinct notch, lower lobe small and pointed

Breeding Internal fertilization: nourishment initially supplied by egg yolk; subsequent nourishment via placenta; gestation around 8 months; litter sizes from 6 to over 40 pups, depending on species and size of female

Diet Wide range of prey from open-water and bottom-dwelling bony fish to skates, rays, other sharks (including hammerheads), squid, crustaceans, and sea snakes

Habitat Open and shallow waters, ranging in depth from inshore reefs and near-shore shallows down to around 1,000 ft (300 m) in scalloped hammerhead; most species stay in upper 260 ft (80 m) of the water column

Distribution Widespread in many tropical and warm-temperate regions

Status IUCN lists at various levels of threat: slender hammerhead (*E. blochii*)—Near Threatened; crown shark (*S. corona*)—Near Threatened; scalloped hammerhead (*S. lewini*)—Lower Risk near threatened; great hammerhead (*S. mokarran*)—Data Deficient; smooth hammerhead (*S. zygaena*)—Lower Risk near threatened; some populations have declined due to uncontrolled fishing

Megamouth Shark

Common name Megamouth shark

Scientific name *Megachasma pelagios*

Family Megachasmidae

Order Lamniformes

Size Largest female known measured 16.9 ft (5.2 m); males probably smaller

Key features Large, bulbous head with short snout; huge mouth with numerous very small teeth; lining of the mouth silvery; tapering body; upper lobe of caudal fin about 1.5 times the length of the lower lobe; body color blackish-brown above; lower half brilliant white; tips of pectoral and pelvic fins white; posterior edges of pectoral, pelvic, dorsal, and anal fins also white

Breeding Fertilization internal; mating in southern California waters may occur in October/November, but not known for certain; no details for other regions; embryos may consume unfertilized eggs during development, but number of pups produced, duration of their period of development, or frequency of broods produced by a female all unknown

Diet Predominantly euphausiid (luminescent deepwater) shrimp, some jellyfish, and other invertebrates

Habitat Midwater (pelagic) zones of the open ocean—hence its specific name, *pelagios*; known to migrate daily from depths of 40 ft (12.1 m) or less to around 545 ft (166 m), but may dive to around 3,300 ft (1,000 m)

Distribution Recorded in Atlantic, Indian, and Pacific Oceans; first caught in 1976 but not described and formally identified as a new species until 1983

Status Listed by IUCN as Data Deficient; world population unknown

Basking Shark

Common name Basking shark (sunfish)

Scientific name *Cetorhinus maximus*

Family Cetorhinidae

Order Lamniformes

Size Around 33 ft (10 m), but possibly up to 50.5 ft (15.4 m)

Key features Variable color—brown, dusky black, or blue along the back, becoming lighter toward dull white belly; snout pointed; mouth cavernous; skin covered in small denticles and thick layer of foul-smelling mucus; 5 large gill slits, inside which is the food-filtering mechanism consisting of gill rakers; caudal fin typically sharklike, with upper lobe longer than lower

Breeding Internal fertilization followed by a gestation period of around 3.5 years; developing embryos believed to feed on unfertilized eggs during gestation; females thought to give birth to 1 or 2 pups measuring about 5.5 ft (1.7 m) in length (although some estimates indicate up to 50 young in a single batch)

Diet Planktonic invertebrates filtered from water by the gill rakers

Habitat Spotted mainly in inshore and offshore surface waters, but suspected of also inhabiting deeper zones, possibly down to 650 ft (198 m) or more

Distribution Temperate regions of Pacific and Atlantic Oceans, extending—along western coast of American continent— from British Columbia to Baja California; on east coast ranges from Newfoundland to South America, perhaps avoiding Caribbean; in eastern Atlantic ranges from Scandinavia to southern Africa; also found in Mediterranean and Black Sea, eastern Indian Ocean, around Australia, New Zealand, and up to Asian coasts, past Japan and northward

Status Listed by IUCN as Vulnerable for the species overall, but Endangered for the north Pacific and northeast Atlantic population; not listed by CITES

Great White Shark

Common name Great white shark (white pointer, blue pointer, maneater, Tommy, death shark, uptail, white death)

Scientific name *Carcharodon carcharias*

Family Lamnidae

Order Lamniformes

Size Specimens in excess of 36 ft (11 m) reported, but confirmed data indicates a maximum size of 18–20 ft (5.5–6.0m)

Key features Torpedo-shaped body with conical, pointed snout; teeth of upper and lower jaws very similar and saw-edged—upper teeth slightly broader; top half of body slate-gray to brownish; irregular line separates top half from pure-white lower half of body; lobes of caudal fin more similar to each other than in most other species, but upper lobe a little larger than lower; underside of pectoral fins have blackish tips

Breeding Livebearing species that gives birth to 5–14 young (probably more) after gestation period of up to a year; scars predominantly on pectoral fins of mature great white females suggest males bite females during mating, as in other sharks

Diet Mainly bony fish; also cartilaginous fish (including other sharks), turtles, seabirds, and marine mammals, including dolphins, seals, and sea lions

Habitat Wide range of habitats from surfline to offshore (but rarely midocean) and from surface down to around depths exceeding 820 ft (250 m)—although it has been reported to dive to a depth of over 4,000 ft (over 1,200 m)

Distribution Predominantly in warm-temperate and subtropical waters, but also warmer areas

Status Listed by IUCN as Vulnerable; world population sometimes quoted at around 10,000, but true numbers unknown

Great-Tooth Sawfish

Common name Great-tooth sawfish (southern sawfish, freshwater sawfish)

Scientific name *Pristis microdon*

Family Pristidae

Order Rajiformes

Size Overall body length recorded up to 46 ft (14 m)

Key features Flat, narrow snout with well-spaced teeth of matching size around its edges, creating an impression of a saw; evident dorsal and caudal fins; first dorsal fin positioned in front of pelvic fins on sides of body; 14–22 pairs of large teeth on each side; swims like a shark; solitary

Breeding Female gives birth to litters of often more than 20 young; breeding period coincides with the rainy season in parts of its range (November to December in northern Queensland); may not breed for the first time until more than 15 years old

Diet Mainly fish; some invertebrates

Habitat Shallow areas of the sea; can also be encountered in estuaries and rivers

Distribution From Africa through the tropical Indo-Pacific region to southeast Asia, north to the Philippines, and south to Australia

Status Listed by IUCN as Endangered; numbers have fallen significantly in recent years as a result of overfishing; heavily hunted as a source of food and for the saws, which are sold as curios; habitat changes, pollution, and relatively low reproductive rate have also contributed to population declines

Thornback Ray

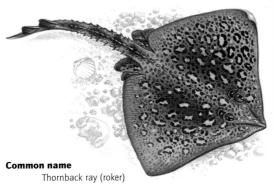

Common name
Thornback ray (roker)

Scientific name *Raja clavata*

Family Rajidae

Order Rajiformes

Size 4 ft (1.2 m)

Key features Short snout with rounded tip, the disk wider than the body; very variable brown coloration on upper body, also blotched with both light and darker markings, may even have a marbled appearance; covered in prickles; undersurface of body is white; tail barred

Breeding During mating male holds female with his claspers and the pair wrap their bodies around each other; female lays up to 20 eggs every day from March to August; oblong eggs up to 3.5 in (9 cm) long and almost 2.75 in (7 cm) in diameter; young thornbacks emerge after about 5 months

Diet Mainly crustaceans; also fish

Habitat Sandy areas, largely on coastal shelf; lives near seabed

Distribution Eastern Atlantic ranging from Iceland and Norway down through the North Sea as far south as Namibia in southwestern Africa, possibly even down to South Africa; also ranges through Mediterranean to Black Sea

Status Listed by IUCN as Lower Risk near threatened; relatively common but heavily fished in places, with some restrictions on catches

Common Stingray

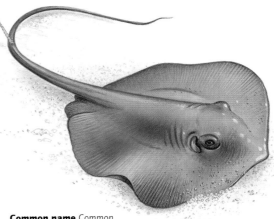

Common name Common stingray

Scientific name *Dasyatis pastinaca*

Family Dasyatidae

Order Rajiformes

Size 2 ft (60 cm)

Key features Relatively broad, triangular front to body; long, narrow tail twice as long as distance between snout and vent; dark color on upper surface, light below; prominent spiracles adjacent to eyes; sharp sting resembling a dagger, measuring up to 14 in (35 cm) long, projects backward from rear portion of tail; sting used for defensive purposes (rather than to capture prey) and delivers neurotoxic venom

Breeding Eggs retained in female's body; she gives birth to 6–9 young after gestation period of about 4 months, during which young are nourished by outgrowths from her uterus

Diet Invertebrates and fish

Habitat Open areas of seabed close to shore; stays close to sandy bottom

Distribution Northeastern Atlantic down to Mediterranean, most common in the west; recorded as far south as coast of Zaire

Status Not threatened; still relatively common but potentially vulnerable, especially where heavily fished; however, 5 other species of *Dasyatis* listed under various categories of threat by the IUCN

Spotted Eagle Ray

Manta Ray

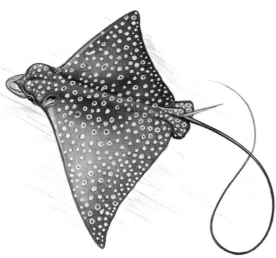

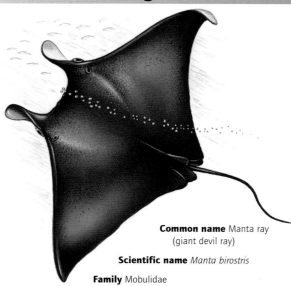

Common name Manta ray
(giant devil ray)

Scientific name *Manta birostris*

Family Mobulidae

Common name Spotted eagle ray

Scientific name *Aetobatus narinari*

Family Myliobatidae

Order Myliobatiformes

Size 6 ft (1.8 m), sometimes even larger

Key features Obviously and relatively even whitish or bluish-white spotted patterning over the dark slatey to chestnut-brown upper surface of the body; underparts predominantly white, extending onto the sides of the face; broad, projecting lower jaw; long, narrow tail up to 3 times the length of body, with inconspicuous stinging spines near the base; active and social by nature

Breeding Receptive female usually mates with several males; mating takes form of embracing each other on underparts to avoid damage by spines; female gives birth to 4 live young after gestation period of about 1 year; young nourished during development by food produced through outgrowths from mother's uterus

Diet Mainly clams, oysters, and crustaceans; digs up prey buried in seabed with spadelike snout; breaks open shells with little effort due to flattened, platelike structure of teeth

Habitat Sandy areas relatively near the coast

Distribution Very extensive, found in temperate and tropical areas of the Atlantic off the coasts of both the Americas, Europe, and Africa; also ranges from the Red Sea into the Indian and Pacific Oceans

Status Listed by IUCN as Data Deficient with no detailed information on populations, although taken as bycatch in fisheries around the world

Order Myliobatiformes

Size 17 ft (5.2 m); Atlantic mantas are largest

Key features Very distinctive horn-shaped projections (cephalic fins) extend down beneath the eyes; blackish-brown on dorsal surface, with a variable white collar whose patterning allows individuals to be identified; whitish on ventral side of body; active by nature, swimming over long distances rather than concealing itself on seabed

Breeding Female gives birth to a single young after gestation period of about 13 months; young well developed at birth, with a wingspan of over 3 ft (1 m)

Diet Typically feeds on plankton; sometimes small fish

Habitat Usually in upper reaches of the ocean; sometimes found in estuaries and even in rivers

Distribution Circumglobal in tropical parts of Atlantic, Indian, and Pacific Oceans; ranges as far south as Brazil, sometimes as far north as New England and Georges Bank on eastern U.S. seaboard, although not consistently recorded north of the Carolinas; occurs northward to Redondo Beach, California, on Pacific Coast

Status Listed by IUCN as Data Deficient; some populations have declined due to fisheries; now very scarce in Gulf of California

Coelacanth

Common name Coelacanth

Scientific names *Latimeria chalumnae, L. menadoensis*

Family Latimeriidae

Order Coelacanthiformes

Number of species 2 known

Size Up to 6 ft (1.8 m) long and weighing up to 210 lb (95 kg)

Form Bluish base color when alive, with light pinkish-white blotches

Breeding Livebearer; a few large eggs, each about 3.5 in (9 cm) in diameter and weighing 10.6–12.4 oz (300–350 g), are released into the oviduct, which acts as a womb for embryos that grow to at least 12 in (30 cm) before birth

Diet Smaller fish

Habitat Cold waters in deep ocean down to more than 330 ft (100 m)

Distribution Cape Province and KwaZulu-Natal (South Africa); Comoro Archipelago (islands between northern tip of Madagascar and east coast of Africa); a related species, *Latimeria menadoensis*, is known from northern Sulawesi, Indonesia

Status Listed by IUCN as Critical with little idea of population; CITES: Appendix I

Lungfish

The Australian lungfish (*Neoceratodus forsteri*) grows to a length of up to 5 feet (1.5 m). A native of northeast Australia, it favors deep, slow-flowing water.

Common name Lungfish

Orders Lepidosireniformes (South American and African lungfish): families Lepidosirenidae (1 sp: South American lungfish, *Lepidosiren paradoxa*) and Protopteridae (4 spp. of African lungfish in genus *Protopterus*); Ceratodontiformes (Australian lungfish): family Ceratodontidae (single sp: *Neoceratodus forsteri*)

Infraclass Dipnoi

Number of species 6

Size From 33 in (85 cm) in spotted lungfish (*P. dolloi*) to over 5 ft (1.5 m) in *Neoceratodus* and over 6.5 ft (2 m) in Ethiopian lungfish (*P. aethiopicus*)

Key features Body elongate with continuous dorsal, caudal, and anal fins; *Neoceratodus* with paddlelike pectoral and pelvic fins and stout body scales; *Lepidosiren* and *Protopterus* with filamentlike pectoral fins, fleshy pelvic fins (filamentlike in *Protopterus*), and smooth scales

Diet Mainly carnivorous, feeding on aquatic animals

Breeding Generally after first rains—before summer rains in Australian lungfish; eggs of African and South American spp. laid in burrows guarded by male, fry have external gills; eggs of Australian lungfish scattered among vegetation, hatch into fry without external gills

Habitat Still pools and deep rivers in Australian lungfish, similar but often shallower waters in other spp.

Distribution Australian lungfish: Murray and Burnett River systems, southwest Queensland, Australia; South American spp: Amazon and Paraná River basins; African spp: widespread in Africa

Status Australian lungfish listed in CITES: Appendix II

Bichirs and Ropefish

The shortfin bichir (*Polypterus palmas palmas*) grows to 12 inches (30 cm) long and feeds mainly on other freshwater aquatic animals. It lives in rivers of Côte d'Ivoire and eastern Liberia.

Common name Bichirs and ropefish

Family   Polypteridae

Order   Polypteriformes

Subclass Chondrostei

Number of species 10 in 2 genera (*Polypterus, Erpetoichthys*)

Size   Smallest: Guinean bichir (*P. ansorgii*) at 11 in (28 cm); largest sp: Congo bichir (*P. endlicheri congicus*) up to 38 in (97 cm)

Key features Elongated body, especially ropefish; head large with flattened front half; snout rounded; eyes small; mouth moderately large; dorsal fin consists of number of finlets with "flag-and-pole" arrangement of spines and rays; pectoral fins with fleshy base; large ganoid body scales; coloration: dull and mottled in many species; attractive dark markings in ornate bichir, with orange-red bands in pectoral fins

Breeding In some species adults move into flooded areas during late summer; individual pairs shed and fertilize 200–300 eggs among vegetation; hatching takes about 4 days; larvae have external gills like amphibian tadpoles

Diet   All are hunters, mainly at night, taking insects, other aquatic invertebrates, frogs, and fish

Habitat Shallow water along the edges of rivers, lakes, swamps, and flooded areas, often close to or among vegetation; also waters that have low oxygen content

Distribution Widespread in tropical and subtropical Africa

Status Not threatened

Baltic or Common Sturgeon

Common name Baltic or common sturgeon (Atlantic sturgeon— this common name also applied to another species: *Acipenser oxyrhynchus*)

Scientific name *Acipenser sturio*

Subfamily Acipenserinae

Family   Acipenseridae

Order   Acipenseriformes

Size   Usually 10–11 ft (3–3.4 m) but up to 20 ft (6 m)

Key features Elongated body with distinct snout and heterocercal caudal fin; 5 rows of large, stout scutes, each with a central "spike," along body; underslung mouth with 2 pairs of barbels; coloration: greenish-brown on the back, yellowish-white below

Breeding Migrates from sea to freshwater spawning grounds; spawning occurs in flowing water over gravel; up to 2.5 million eggs abandoned and hatch in less than 1 week; adults return to sea after spawning; juveniles spend up to 4 years in fresh water prior to migrating to sea

Diet   Bottom-dwelling marine invertebrates and small fish; does not feed during spawning period

Habitat Mainly shallow coastal waters, usually over sand or mud; some move to deeper waters

Distribution Atlantic Ocean from Norway to North Africa and into western Mediterranean, Baltic, and Black Seas; 1 landlocked population in Lake Ladoga near Leningrad, Russia

Status Listed by IUCN as Critically Endangered; CITES Appendix I; close to extinction in parts of range due to overfishing, accidental catches, pollution, and loss of habitat

Beluga

Common name Beluga

Scientific name *Huso huso*

Subfamily Acipenserinae

Family Acipenseridae

Order Acipenseriformes

Size Up to 28 ft (8.6 m) and 2,865 lb (1,300 kg); typical large specimens up to 20 ft (6 m)

Key features Heavy-bodied profile in adults; younger specimens more streamlined; skin membranes bordering gills fused in throat area; wide mouth and 2 pairs of long barbels on snout; scutes not particularly strong and become worn down and partially lost with age

Breeding "Fall" race migrates 300 mi (500 km) or more in September–October to upper reaches of rivers; "spring" race migrates in March–April to middle and lower reaches; both spawn around May over pebble or gravel; up to 7 million eggs laid by a large female; fry hatch in about 1 week; adults return to the sea; juveniles generally move out to sea during their first year

Diet Young beluga feed on invertebrates and small fish; adults feed almost exclusively on fish plus other prey, including waterfowl and, reportedly, seals

Habitat Mainly close to the surface or in midwater regions over fine sediments, often close to estuaries; moves to deeper water during winter—as deep as 590 ft (180 m) in Black Sea

Distribution Adriatic, Black, and Caspian Seas, and associated river systems

Status Some populations classified by IUCN as Endangered; Sea of Azov stock listed as Critically Endangered and Adriatic stock as Extinct; CITES: Appendix II

American Paddlefish

Common name American paddlefish

Scientific name *Polyodon spathula*

Family Polyodontidae

Order Acipenseriformes

Size Can attain more than 6.6 ft (2 m) in length and over 100 lb (45 kg) in weight; females larger than males

Key features Body elongate and sharklike with unique "paddle" accounting for a third of total length; cavernous mouth; coloration: slate-gray above, often mottled, shading to lighter tones below

Breeding Spawns in April and May, producing up to 750,000 large eggs that hatch in about 1 week; fry free-swimming from the outset

Diet Small drifting invertebrates (zooplankton) and insect larvae; feeds by swimming with huge mouth gaping open and filtering organisms from water with its sievelike gill rakers

Habitat Slow-flowing waters such as oxbow lakes and backwaters more than 4 ft (1.2 m) deep

Distribution North America mainly in Missouri River basin and Gulf slope drainage

Status Listed by IUCN as Vulnerable due to habitat alteration, pollution, and overfishing (the latter especially in the 1980s, when paddlefish were poached for caviar to address shortfall in supplies of sturgeon caviar from war-torn Iran); CITES Appendix II

Longnose Gar

Common name Longnose gar

Scientific name *Lepisosteus osseus*

Family Lepisosteidae

Order Semionotiformes

Size Up to 6 ft (1.8 m)

Key features Somewhat reptilian in appearance, resembling the long-snouted Asian crocodile (gharial); slender-bodied; narrow, long snout (longest of any gar in relation to head and body); ganoid scales; abbreviated heterocercal tail

Breeding Migrates upriver in early spring; spawning can occur as early as March and extend through summer to August depending on locality; single female may spawn with several males in depression, laying 27,000–77,000 eggs; fry hatch in 6–9 days and adhere to vegetation until yolk sac consumed; males mature at 3–4 years; females may take 6 years.

Diet Predatory, mainly on fish and crustaceans

Habitat Clear, still, or slow-moving waters, including lakes, rivers, and backwaters; often close to vegetation or submerged branches; occurs in brackish water in coastal areas

Distribution Widely distributed from Quebec, Canada, south to central Florida and from Delaware westward to Mexico; also Great Lakes, except Lake Superior

Status Not threatened

Bowfin

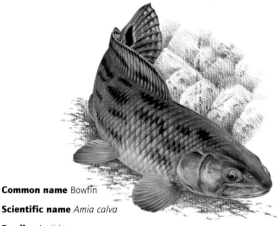

Common name Bowfin

Scientific name *Amia calva*

Family Amiidae

Order Amiiformes

Size Up to 43 in (1.1 m) long and 9 lb (4 kg) in weight

Key features Large head with 2 forward-pointing barbels on snout; sturdy cylindrical body with long-based dorsal fin with some 48 rays; cycloid scales; abbreviated heterocercal tail; coloration: adults dark and drab with a faded eyespot near the base of the top tail fin rays (a black spot surrounded by yellow-orange halo), often barely visible; in juveniles eyespot and halo are brilliantly colored, forming a "false eye" that draws predators' attention away from the head

Breeding In spring; male migrates to shallow water and builds circular matted depression up to 24 in (61 cm) across, often close to tree roots or submerged logs; female lays up to 30,000 eggs that hatch in 8–10 days; eggs and young defended by male for up to 4 months; young grow relatively slowly and may not mature until they are 3–5 years old

Diet Worms, crustaceans, fish, reptiles, and small mammals; juveniles eat plankton, aquatic insects, and planktonic crustaceans

Habitat Lakes, still and slow-moving waters, including swamps; usually near vegetation

Distribution Widespread in eastern North America

Status Not threatened

European and American Eels

The 4.3-foot (1.3-m) European eel (*Anguilla anguilla*) occurs in fresh water in Europe and North Africa, as well as on North Atlantic coasts from Iceland to North Africa and the Mediterranean and Black Seas.

Common name European and American eels

Family Anguillidae

Order Anguilliformes

Number of species 15 in 1 genus (*Anguilla*)

Size Typically up to 3.3 ft (1 m)

Key features Snakelike body; crescentlike gill openings on sides of head, broadening into the base of the relatively large pectoral fin; tiny scales evident on body; complete lateral line extending down both sides of head and body; underside of body lightens from golden yellow to silvery as it matures, with upperparts becoming black; have a strong migratory urge when adult, returning to the sea at this stage; otherwise lives often in slow-flowing stretches of fresh water

Breeding Females lay eggs which hatch into larvae that do not resemble adults

Diet Invertebrates and smaller fish eaten in fresh water

Habitat Young hatch in sea; move to fresh water and return to marine environment to breed themselves (behavior described as "catadromous")

Distribution Widely in much of Europe from the far north down throughout the Mediterranean region (European eel, *A. anguilla*); eastern North America from Labrador down to northern South America (American eel, *A. rostrata*)

Status Both groups are numerous, although numbers have declined significantly in some areas

False Moray Eels

The 7-inch (18-cm) seagrass eel (*Chilorhinus suensonii*) lives in the tropical waters of the western Atlantic from Bermuda and southern Florida south to Brazil. It inhabits sandy areas and seagrass beds, and feeds on small fish and invertebrates.

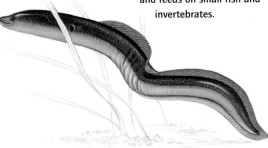

Common name False moray eels

Family Chlopsidae (Xenocongridae)

Order Anguilliformes

Number of species 24 in 9 genera

Size From 6.5 in (16 cm) in collared eel (*Kaupichthys nuchalis*) to 16.5 in (42 cm) in bicolored false moray eel (*Chlopsis bicolor*)

Key features Posterior nostril opening present in lip, with small, rounded gill openings; pores (connecting to lateral line to provide sensory information) present on head but not on body; pectoral fins absent in most species; brown coloration; white inside mouth

Breeding Presumed egg laying; young go through leptocephalus phase; no other details known

Diet Probably invertebrates and small fish

Habitat Marine environment, especially shallow water and reefs

Distribution Predominantly tropical and subtropical parts of Atlantic, Indian, and Pacific Oceans, especially around islands from Seychelles to Hawaii; bicolored false moray eel ranges from coast of Florida to Mediterranean region

Status Unclear; currently not considered under threat

Moray Eels

The 5-foot (1.5-m) undulated moray eel (*Gymnothorax undulatus*) lives on rocky reef flats in the Indo-Pacific from the Red Sea and East Africa to French Polynesia, north to southern Japan and Hawaii, south to Australia's Great Barrier Reef, and east to Costa Rica and Panama.

Common name Moray eels

Family Muraenidae

Order Anguilliformes

Number of species About 200 in around 15 genera

Size Largest species recorded (giant moray, *Gymnothorax javanicus*) up to 10 ft (3 m)

Key features Sharp, pointed teeth to grasp small active prey, with a double row of teeth on pharyngeal bones in most species; much blunter dentition pattern for crushing shells in crab-eating morays; some grow to large size and also may be brightly colored; dorsal and anal fins often prominent, but fins reduced to tip of the tail, fusing with caudal fin, in *Gymnomuraena*; tail and head are similar in length; live in lairs rather than in open; often prefer to hunt at night, grabbing unsuspecting prey venturing within reach

Breeding Undocumented, but goes through leptocephalus phase

Diet Carnivorous; techniques to capture prey vary; chain moray (*Echidna catenata*) frequently hunts crabs out of water at low tide

Habitat Relatively shallow waters, usually found in warmer seas associated with reefs; at least 2 species venture into fresh water; only 1 species occurs north of the Mediterranean

Distribution Found in all oceans of the world

Status Generally common

Snipe Eels

The 29.3-inch (74.5-cm) avocet snipe eel (*Avocettina infans*) occurs between 165 and 15,000 feet (50–4,570 m) in all oceans north of about 20° S—including the eastern Pacific from Canada's Queen Charlotte Islands down to central Mexico, but excluding the Mediterranean and the eastern equatorial Pacific.

Common name Snipe eels

Family Nemichthyidae

Order Anguilliformes

Number of species 9 in 3 genera

Size Longest species grow to over 3.3 feet (1 m)

Key features Exceedingly slender, long jaws, with upper longer than lower; jaws much shorter in mature males; jaws also diverge along their length; similarly slender body with large eyes; dorsal and anal fins joined with caudal fin; supraoccipital bone absent from skull; others may be as well, including the pterygoid and palatine; inactive, specialized hunter of small invertebrate prey

Breeding Females lay eggs; spawning is an apparently communal occurrence

Diet Crustaceans, particularly deep-sea shrimp; possibly ectoparasites of other fish; not active hunters; lie vertically in water with open mouth, awaiting passing prey

Habitat Restricted to marine environment, typically at depths from about 5,250 to 16,400 ft (1,600–5,000 m)

Distribution Widely distributed throughout world's oceans; more common in warmer waters but recorded in the Atlantic as far north as Sable Island Bank off Nova Scotia and between Iceland and the Faeroe Islands

Status Probably not especially rare

Conger Eels

The 10-foot (3-m) European conger eel (*Conger conger*) occurs in the eastern Atlantic from Iceland south to Senegal, including the Mediterranean and Black Seas, down to a depth of 1,640 feet (500 m) deep. Found on rocky or sandy bottoms, it moves from the coast into deeper water when an adult.

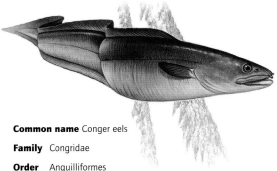

Common name Conger eels

Family Congridae

Order Anguilliformes

Number of species 150 in 32 genera

Size Largest species recorded at up to 10 ft (3 m)

Key features Even young congers have a dorsal fin that starts above the pectoral fins, extending right down the length of the body; upper jaw protrudes beyond lower, both equipped with large, powerful teeth; no scales evident on skin; capable of adjusting color to match surroundings from grayish-brown upper parts in sandy areas to darker color in rocky crevices

Breeding Essentially undocumented, but pass through a leptocephalus phase; appear to migrate to spawning grounds, e.g., Sargasso Sea; females may produce up to 8 million eggs

Diet Carnivorous; active and aggressive, taking fish and cephalopods unawares

Habitat Often associated with wrecks, reefs, or rocky areas on the seabed

Distribution Atlantic, Pacific, and Indian Oceans

Status Common

Swallower, Gulper, and Pelican Eels

The 3.3-foot (1-m) pelican eel (*Eurypharynx pelecanoides*) is a deepwater species ranging between 1,640 and 24,600 feet (500–7,500 m). It occurs in the eastern Pacific from northern California to Peru. Its mouth is greatly enlarged by a backward extension of its jaws; it feeds mainly on crustaceans.

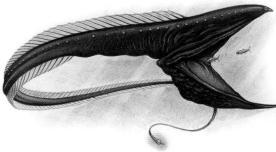

Common name Swallower, gulper, and pelican eels

Families Saccopharyngidae, Monognathidae, Eurypharyngidae

Order Saccopharyngiformes

Number of species 24 in 3 genera

Size From 6.3 in (16 cm) to 6.5 ft (2 m)

Key features All species have a very large mouth and gape, with a distending pharynx, enabling them to swallow correspondingly large prey without apparent difficulty; long, slender tail, often equipped with light-emitting organs; pelican eel (*Eurypharynx pelecanoides*) is unique, being the only bony fish to have 5 gill arches with 6 visceral clefts; vertebral count typically between 100 and 300 bones; swim bladder present; no scales on body

Breeding It is thought that these eels only spawn once in their lifetime, with both males and females dying soon afterward

Diet Fish and other creatures living at great depths

Habitat Deep marine waters

Distribution Widely distributed throughout Atlantic, Pacific, and Indian Oceans

Status Not under any apparent immediate threat from deep-sea fishing

Atlantic Tarpon

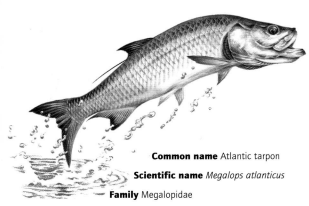

Common name Atlantic tarpon

Scientific name *Megalops atlanticus*

Family Megalopidae

Order Elopiformes

Size Up to 8.25 ft (2.5 m)

Key features Elongated, flattened body shape; large eyes; lower jaw extends forward from behind eyes; well-forked caudal fin with a threadlike projection on last ray of dorsal fin; large silvery scales with a slight metallic blue coloration over the back; small, sharp teeth throughout oral cavity; active, lively fish, often congregating in groups where food supply is plentiful, but not a schooling species; frequently leaps out of water

Breeding Spawns in shallow waters, producing up to 12 million eggs; young hatch into ribbonlike leptocephali that subsequently develop in brackish or even fresh water where they are able to breathe atmospheric oxygen directly, which helps them survive in poorly oxygenated waters (adults also have ability to breathe atmospheric oxygen); onset of sexual maturity relatively slow at 7–13 years, when they reach 4 ft (1.2 m) long

Diet Carnivorous; primarily fish and cephalopods

Habitat Reef-associated; in fresh, brackish or marine waters; older tarpon sometimes found in rivers

Distribution Western Atlantic, mainly in tropical seas from North Carolina down to Brazil; occasionally recorded farther north up to Nova Scotia; also eastern Atlantic from Senegal to Angola, exceptional occurrences in Portugal, the Azores, and France's Atlantic coast

Status Not under immediate threat

Arapaima

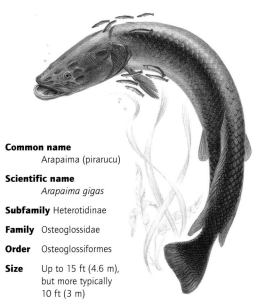

Common name Arapaima (pirarucu)

Scientific name *Arapaima gigas*

Subfamily Heterotidinae

Family Osteoglossidae

Order Osteoglossiformes

Size Up to 15 ft (4.6 m), but more typically 10 ft (3 m)

Key features Long, powerful body; almost cylindrical in central portion; flattened head with large eyes and cavernous upturned mouth; coloration: variable with grayish, greenish, and bluish hues, and large purple-edged scales, particularly along back; fins have reddish tinge

Breeding October–May depending on location; pair spawn above shallow depression dug in lake or river bed; between 4,000 and 47,000 eggs are laid and incubated in mouth by one parent (probably male), which develops white tubercles on snout; they may produce a nutritious secretion for the fry following release

Diet Mainly fish but also other aquatic vertebrates and even birds

Habitat Large bodies of water, which may be seasonally oxygen deficient; to compensate can gulp air at water surface and then absorb oxygen into the network of blood vessels surrounding swim bladder

Distribution Amazonia

Status Listed as Data Deficient by IUCN; CITES Appendix II; population low or extinct in certain areas owing to heavy fishing, habitat loss, and pollution; captive-breeding programs in operation both for local food source and to satisfy demand for aquarium fish

DragonFish

African Knifefish

The false featherfin (*Xenomystus nigri*) is distinguished from the other African knifefish by its lack of a dorsal fin. It is also smaller, growing to a maximum of 12 inches (30 cm) long.

Common name Dragonfish (golden dragonfish, Asian arowana, Asian bonytongue)

Scientific name *Scleropages formosus*

Subfamily Osteoglossinae

Family Osteoglossidae

Order Osteoglossiformes

Size Up to 35 in (89 cm); usually smaller

Key features Compressed, torpedo-shaped body with pointed head; large eyes and mouth; 2 chin barbels; body covered in large, stout scales; 3 main wild color forms: red, gold, and green or silver

Breeding Mating July–December, preceded by long period of courtship and bonding that can last 2–3 months; 30–90 eggs incubated in mouth of male for 5–6 weeks, by which time the fry may be nearly 3.5 in (9 cm) long

Diet Wide range of invertebrates and small vertebrates; feeds mainly at or near water surface but will leap up and snatch prey from overhanging vegetation

Habitat Still or slow-flowing waters that are often turbid or heavily vegetated

Distribution Cambodia, Laos, Vietnam, peninsular Malaysia, Philippines, Indonesia (Kalimantan and Sumatra); introduced to Singapore

Status Listed as Endangered by IUCN; CITES Appendix I

Common name African knifefish

Scientific names *Papyrocranus*, *Xenomystus* spp.

Family Notopteridae

Order Osteoglossiformes

Number of species 3 in 2 genera

Size African featherfin, or African knifefish (*Papyrocranus afer*), up to 32 in (80 cm); *P. congoensis* up to 32 in (80 cm); false featherfin, or African knifefish (*Xenomystus nigri*), up to 12 in (30 cm)

Key features All 3 species have compressed, elongated bodies with large eyes and mouth and characteristic knifelike anal fin joined to small caudal fin; *Xenomystus* has long, tubelike nasal openings; *Papyrocranus* species have small dorsal fin but no pelvics; *Xenomystus* does not have a dorsal fin but has pelvic fins

Breeding *Xenomystus* lays up to 200 eggs, but no details of brood care available; breeding details of *Papyrocranus* not known

Diet Mainly aquatic invertebrates plus flying insects that fall into the water; also take fish

Habitat Mostly relatively quiet waters, often with heavy vegetation and shade

Distribution *Papyrocranus afer* western Sierra Leone to Niger River; *P. congoensis* Congo River; *Xenomystus nigri* widely distributed from West Africa to Nile River

Status Not threatened

Elephantnoses and Whales

The down poker (*Campylomormyrus rhynchophorus*) is a native of the Congo basin in Central Africa, where it grows to 8.5 inches (22 cm) in length.

Common name Elephantnoses and whales

Family Mormyridae

Order Osteoglossiformes

Number of species Around 200 in 18 genera

Size From 3.5 in (9 cm) to 20 in (50 cm)

Key features Laterally compressed body with dorsal, anal, pelvic, and caudal fins well formed; long, narrow extension from back of dorsal and anal fins to base of caudal fin (known as caudal peduncle) and deeply forked tail; mouth extremely variable, ranging from lower lip extended into proboscis or trunk to long snout with small mouth at tip or underslung mouth beneath rounded snout; eyes relatively small; moves and detects prey, food, and mates in dark or murky water by producing weak electrical current from caudal peduncle; pulses bounce off objects, and echoes picked up by receptors in head and front of body

Breeding No details available; differently shaped anal fins in males and females of some species may indicate that close proximity is necessary for effective egg fertilization

Diet Mainly worms and other bottom-living invertebrates

Habitat Frequently in turbid waters with muddy bottoms, often with submerged and above-water vegetation, e.g., shady marshes

Distribution Widely distributed in tropical Africa and the Nile River

Status Not threatened

Aba Aba

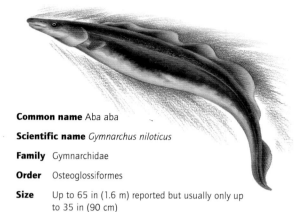

Common name Aba aba

Scientific name *Gymnarchus niloticus*

Family Gymnarchidae

Order Osteoglossiformes

Size Up to 65 in (1.6 m) reported but usually only up to 35 in (90 cm)

Key features Elongated body; relatively large, tapering head with rounded snout; large underslung mouth; small eyes; no pelvic, anal, or caudal fins; dorsal fin with extremely long base containing 183–230 rays; coloration: dark gray along top half, fading to whitish along belly with small dark spots; albinos occasionally reported; weak electric current generated in muscle cells (known as Sach's organ) toward the back of the body help the fish navigate, locate prey, and detect other fish in murky waters

Breeding Builds large elliptical floating nest around 39 in (1 m) in densely vegetated areas like swamps; lays around 1,000 amber-colored eggs; nest guarded by one or possibly both parents; hatching takes about 5 days

Diet Insects, crustaceans, and fish taken at all depths

Habitat Slow-flowing or still waters such as swamps, often with muddy bottoms and turbid water

Distribution Tropical Africa including the Gambia, Nile, Niger, Volta, and Senegal River systems; also Lake Chad and Lake Turkana (Rudolf)

Status Not threatened

Anchovies

The 8-inch (20-cm) Peruvian anchovy (*Engraulis ringens*) occurs in the South Pacific from Peru to Chile at depths between 10 and 260 feet (3–80 m); it stays within 50 miles (80 km) of the coast. The fish is a filter feeder, entirely dependent on the rich plankton found in the Peru Current.

Common name Anchovies

Family Engraulidae

Order Clupeiformes

Number of species About 140 species in 16 genera

Size Up to about 16 in (40 cm) long, but most species much smaller

Key features Small, slender, silvery fish, longer and thinner than herring and rounder in cross section; large snout gives chinless appearance; single, tall dorsal fin halfway along body; symmetrical forked tail; single anal fin; small paired fins; highly gregarious schooling fish; migrate in search of food and spawning areas

Breeding Large, floating, oval eggs produced in spring

Diet Plankton or small prey collected on gill rakers or grasped with small teeth

Habitat Mostly marine in tropical, subtropical, and temperate waters; about 15 percent of all species live in fresh or brackish water

Distribution Atlantic, Pacific, and Indian Oceans and some adjoining seas and rivers

Status Generally not threatened, but many species are fished intensively and need careful monitoring; IUCN lists freshwater anchovy (*Thryssa scratchleyi*) from Australia as Data Deficient; major fisheries include the Pacific anchovy (*Engraulis mordax*), Peruvian anchovy (*E. ringens*), Japanese anchovy (*E. japonica*), and the European anchovy (*E. encrasicolus*)

Herring

The 10-inch (25-cm) pilchard, or European sardine (*Sardina pilchardus*), occurs in the northeast Atlantic and adjoining seas. It feeds on small crustaceans and other zooplankton.

Common name Herring (pilchards, menhadens, sardines, sprats, shad)

Family Clupeidae

Order Clupeiformes

Number of species About 180 species in 56 genera

Size Mostly small fish less than 20 in (50 cm) long; occasionally up to 5 ft (1.5 cm)

Key features Medium-sized, silvery fish with counter shading (dark on back, pale on underside); pelvic fins exactly opposite dorsal fin located along ventral midline; low dorsal fin about halfway along back; forked and notched tail; highly gregarious schooling fish

Breeding Spawn in school at any time of year depending on population; eggs sink and adhere to seafloor; larvae hatch after a week or more; no parental care

Diet Plankton, especially copepods; occasionally fish larvae; food sieved from water and trapped in gill rakers (appendages that partially block the space between mouth and gills)

Habitat Mostly marine and highly migratory; some species migrate into fresh water, others live permanently in rivers or lakes

Distribution Oceans, seas, and rivers worldwide, especially in coastal areas

Status IUCN lists 14 species in family as having various levels of threat: Alabama shad (*Alosa alabamae*) from the U.S. and *Tenualosa thibaudeaui* from Southeast Asia are listed as Endangered. Main species subject of major fisheries are Atlantic herring (*Clupea harengus*), Pacific herring (*C. pallasii*), sprat (*C. sprattus*), Pacific sardine (*Sardinops sagax*), and pilchard (*Sardina pilchardus*)

Electric Eel

Common name Electric eel (electric knifefish)

Scientific name *Electrophorus electricus*

Family Electrophoridae

Order Gymnotiformes

Size Grows up to 8 ft (2.4 m) long

Key features Large throat; cylindrical teeth; no scales on rounded body; no pelvic fins; anal fin extends around end of tail; approximately 240 vertebrae; remarkable rregenerative powers if injured; can breathe atmospheric air directly; eyes very small relative to body size; prominent electrical organs used to kill prey and to defend itself as well as for communicating via electrical impulses; power generated is enough to kill an animal as big as a horse

Breeding Courtship and egg-laying behavior unknown; males reveal their presence by emitting regular, far-reaching electrical pulses and recognize the shorter responding pulses given off by receptive females

Diet Carnivorous, including shrimp, amphibians, and fish; stuns or kills prey by electrical discharges that can extend up to 3 ft (1 m) in the water; usually hunts after dark

Habitat Confined entirely to fresh water

Distribution Occurs in the Amazon and Orinoco River basins in South America, including Peru, Venezuela, Brazil, and Guyana

Status Not threatened

Barbs

The rosy barb (*Barbus* [*Puntius*] *conchonius*), native to Africa and Europe, is usually about 4 in (10 cm) in length and can be found in both fast- and slow-moving waters.

Common name Barbs

Scientific name *Barbus* spp. (including *Copoëta*, *Puntius*, and *Barbodes*)

Subfamily Cyprininae

Family Cyprinidae

Order Cypriniformes

Number of species About 700

Size From about 1.2 in (3 cm) to about 14 in (35 cm); most species under 4 in (10 cm)

Key features Most species have a laterally compressed body, being deepest (from top to bottom) in region of dorsal fin; head usually oval shaped and scaleless; 2–4 fine barbels around mouth; jaws can be extended forward when opened; dorsal fin located about halfway along back; anal fin small; well-formed caudal fin; lateral line runs along midline of body or slightly above it

Breeding Sticky eggs scattered among plants or over the substratum and then abandoned; hatching may take 1 day but usually takes more than 2 days

Diet Plants, aquatic invertebrates, and insects; larger species also eat small fish

Habitat Wide range of habitats from clear, flowing mountain rivers and streams to lowland water courses, ditches, canals, and flooded fields

Distribution *Barbus* found in Africa and Europe; *Capoëta* found in North Africa and the Near East; *Puntius* widely distributed in southern Asia; *Barbodes* mainly in Indonesia and Sulawesi

Status IUCN lists at least 14 species as Critically Endangered, 4 Endangered, with list growing; over 50 species are considered under some form of threat mainly due to habitat pollution

Common Carp

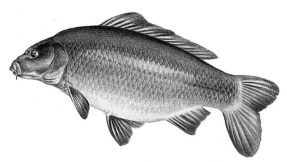

Common name Common carp (European carp, koi)

Scientific name *Cyprinus carpio carpio*; there are also several naturally occurring varieties regarded as subspecies

Subfamily Cyprininae

Family Cyprinidae

Order Cypriniformes

Size Up to around 4 ft (1.2 m) or more in length and a weight of around 82 lb (37.3 kg), but usually smaller

Key features Heavy-bodied fish; fully scaled body; scaleless head with underslung mouth bearing 2 pairs of barbels; well-formed fins; coloration variable but usually greenish-brown on back fading to yellowish-creamish along belly; ornamental varieties (particularly of koi) exhibit wide range of colors

Breeding Season extends from spring into summer; over 1,660,000 sticky eggs scattered among vegetation in shallow water; no parental care; hatching takes 5–8 days

Diet Varied, including vegetation, bottom-living invertebrates, and insects

Habitat Wide range of habitats, particularly larger, slow-flowing or still bodies of water; can tolerate some salt in water; preferred temperature range 37–95°F (3–35°C)

Distribution From its initial central Asian origins the species is now found almost worldwide

Status Although the species *C. carpio* is under no threat of extinction, some of the River Danube populations in a number of countries, e.g., Austria, Hungary, and Romania, are regarded as Critically Endangered; main causes are decreases in range and decline in habitat quality caused by pollutants and other environmental factors; throughout range exploited as food and sport fish, and in some places regarded as a pest due to destruction of plant growth

Goldfish

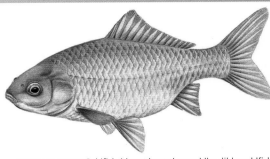

Common name Goldfish (throughout the world); edible goldfish (Malaysia); gibel carp (Kazakhstan); gold crucian carp (Taiwan); golden carp and native carp (Australia)

Scientific name *Carassius auratus auratus*

Subfamily Cyprininae

Family Cyprinidae

Order Cypriniformes

Size Maximum length 23.2 in (59 cm); usually considerably smaller and lighter

Key features Robust, fully scaled body with scaleless head, which is roughly triangular in outline; dorsal fin with 3–4 spines and 15–19 soft rays; anal fin with 2–3 spines and 4–7 soft rays; all fins well formed; no barbels; range of colors—mainly olive-brown to olive-green, but grays, silvers, yellows, golds (with or without blotches), and others also known in wild populations; ornamental varieties exhibit a wide range of colors, finnage, and body shapes

Breeding Many thousands of sticky eggs produced and scattered among vegetation between spring and summer; hatching can take up to 1 week depending on temperature; breeding may involve gynogenesis (stimulation of egg development without fertilization taking place)

Diet Wide-ranging menu, including vegetation and small invertebrates

Habitat Found in a wide range of waters, including lakes, rivers, and ditches; still or slow-flowing waters are preferred, particularly those with soft sediments on the bottom

Distribution Originally from Central Asia, China, and Japan, but introduced virtually throughout the world

Status Not threatened

Gudgeon

Common name Gudgeon

Scientific name *Gobio gobio*

Subfamily Gobioninae

Family Cyprinidae

Order Cypriniformes

Size Up to 8 in (20 cm) but usually smaller

Key features Slim bodied with largish, pointed scaleless head; mouth subterminal; 1 pair of barbels; back slightly curved; belly flat; well-formed fins, especially the forked caudal; no adipose fin; coloration variable throughout range but basically greenish-brown on the back with spotting, fading to yellowish down sides and onto belly, which can have a purplish sheen; row of dark, roundish blotches along center line of body extending from behind gills to base of tail; fins heavily spotted

Breeding Spawning occurs in spring and summer (April–June); several spawnings can occur in favorable locations; up to 3,000 eggs—but often as few as 800—can be laid in small batches over several days; hatching takes 6–20 days depending on temperature

Diet Predominantly bottom-living invertebrates

Habitat Inhabits variety of waters from fast-flowing rivers and streams with sandy or gravelly bottoms to slow-flowing lowland rivers and larger bodies of still waters, such as lakes and reservoirs

Distribution Naturally distributed throughout Europe, except Ireland, Spain, Portugal, southern Italy, Greece, and parts of Scandinavia; it has, however, been introduced into most of these locations, as well as Morocco; natural distribution extends eastward well into the former U.S.S.R.

Status Not threatened

Danios, Rasboras, and Allies

The zebra danio (*Danio rerio*), native to Southeast Asia, Indonesia, and India, is mostly found in shallow waters. Length to 2.4 inches (6 cm).

Common name Danios, rasboras, and allies

Subfamily Rasborinae (Danioninae)—part

Family Cyprinidae

Order Cypriniformes

Number of species Around 245 in about 25 genera

Size From approximately 0.4 in (1 cm) to 7 in (18 cm)

Key features Most species slim bodied; exceptions include harlequin and fire, golden, or pearly rasbora (*Rasbora vaterifloris*); danios and rasboras carry fine barbels around mouth; fins generally well formed; coloration often silvery based with superimposed patterns

Breeding Most species egg scatterers with appetite for own eggs; a few species deposit eggs on a prepared site, usually the underside of a broad leaf; no parental care is known; hatching takes from 1 to several days

Diet Feeds predominantly on small invertebrates, including flying insects

Habitat Mostly shallow waters in a wide range of habitats, from hill streams to lowland rivers; often found in smaller rivulets and streams, mostly with flowing water

Distribution Widely distributed, mainly in Southeast Asia, Indonesia, and India, with lesser distribution in Africa, China, Amur basin, Japan, and Korea; only 1 species of hill trout, *Barilius mesopotamicus*, found in southwestern Eurasia

Status IUCN lists barred danio (*Danio pathirana*) as Critically Endangered; *R. tawarensis* and *R. wilpita* Endangered; fire rasbora (*R. vaterifloris*) Lower Risk conservation dependent

Bitterlings

Minnows and Dace

Bitterlings (*Rhodeus sericeus*), native to mainland Europe and eastern Asia, have an original way of breeding—they lay their eggs inside a freshwater mussel. Length to 4.3 inches (11 cm).

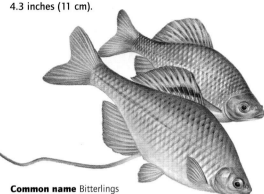

Common name Bitterlings

Subfamily Acheilognathinae

Family Cyprinidae

Order Cypriniformes

Number of species About 15 in 5 genera

Size Most species 2.4–4 in (6–10 cm)

Key features Relatively deep bodied (particularly males); largish silvery scales on body; scaleless head; narrow caudal peduncle; all fins well developed, especially dorsal (in males) and forked caudal fin; coloration: most olive-green on back with silvery scales on sides of body; scales suffused with range of colors

Breeding Generally spawn April–June; eggs usually laid inside freshwater mussel

Diet Wide range of small invertebrates taken both from midwater and bottom zones

Habitat Ponds, lakes, and backwaters of lowland rivers with slow-flowing currents, usually over fine-grained substrata and in vegetated areas; may also occur in more open habitats in turbid water

Distribution Subfamily as a whole ranges from mainland Europe to eastern Asia, including Russia, China, and Japan; some species have been introduced into countries outside their natural range—*Rhodeus sericeus*, for example, now found in U.S., Canada, Britain, Italy, Croatia, and Uzbekistan, while *R. ocellatus ocellatus* has been introduced into China, Japan, Fiji, Korea, and Uzbekistan

Status IUCN lists deepbody bitterling (*Acheilognathus longipinnis*) from central and southern Japan and the Tokyo bitterling (*Tanakia tanago*) from the Kanto Mountains (also in Japan) as Vulnerable; and *A. elongatus* from Lake Dianchi, China, as Endangered

The European minnow (*Phoxinus phoxinus*) can grow to about 4.5 inches (11.5 cm), but is usually smaller. The dace (*Leuciscus leuciscus*) can reach nearly 12 inches (30.5 cm).

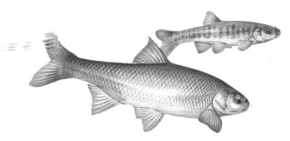

Common name Minnows and dace

Scientific names *Phoxinus, Pimephales, Leuciscus* and other genera

Subfamily Leuciscinae

Family Cyprinidae

Order Cypriniformes

Number of species Around 150 in about 25–30 genera

Size From 2.8 in (7 cm) to 31.5 in (80 cm)

Key features Streamlined body; well-formed eyes; scaleless head; no barbels; well-formed fins; no adipose fin; no true spines on fins

Breeding Eggs usually scattered among vegetation or over rocks, gravel, or sand; usually no parental care; prespawning migrations in many species, with mating taking place in shallow water

Diet From small aquatic invertebrates and insects in smaller species to fish, frogs, and crayfish in larger ones; some plant material also eaten

Habitat Wide range of habitats, including fast-flowing rivers with rocky bottoms and lowland slow-flowing, silt-bottomed waters; almost exclusively fresh water, except European chub (*Leuciscus cephalus*) and some roaches (*Rutilus* spp.)

Distribution North American landmass and Eurasia, with the exception of India and southeastern Asia

Status IUCN lists at least 3 species of *Phoxinus* and 11 species of *Leuciscus* as under threat, including Turskyi dace (*L. turskyi*), probably Extinct

North American Suckers

The razorback sucker (*Xyrauchen texanus*), once extremely abundant in the U.S., is now in danger of extinction. Length to 36 inches (91 cm).

Common name North American suckers

Subfamilies Cycleptinae (part), Letiobinae, Catostominae

Family Catostomidae

Order Cypriniformes

Number of species 68 in about 13 genera

Size From around 6.5 in (16.5 cm) to 40 in (1 m)

Key features Body generally long and relatively slim but highbacked in a few species; head scaleless; underslung mouth and fleshy lips wrinkled or bear papillae except in extinct harelip sucker (*Moxostoma lacerum*); no lip teeth; well-formed dorsal fin with long base in buffaloes (*Ictiobus* spp.), quillback (*Carpiodes cyprinus*), carpsuckers (*C. carpio* and *C. velifer*), and blue sucker (*Cycleptus elongatus*); no adipose fin; well-formed tail

Breeding Spring upriver spawning migrations reported for many species; eggs usually scattered in shallow water and often over pebbles or gravel; no parental care reported

Diet Mostly small invertebrates filtered from bottom sediments and "vacuumed up" with fleshy-lipped, suckerlike mouth

Habitat Most species occur in cool running waters, often with rocky bottoms, in small or medium-sized rivers, or in clear pools; some *Catostomus* species prefer shallower mud- or soft-bottomed pools and creeks; a few occur in lakes, swamps, and ponds with muddy, silty, or sandy bottoms

Distribution Majority exclusively in U.S. and Canada; others extend into Mexico; longnose sucker (*Catostomus catostomus*) also in Siberia

Status IUCN lists nearly 30 species as under varying levels of threat; at least 2 species—Snake River sucker (*Chasmistes muriei*) and harelip sucker (*Moxostoma lacerum*) driven to extinction over past century or so

Clown Loach

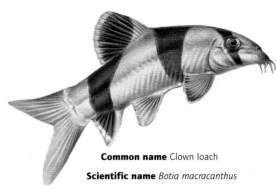

Common name Clown loach

Scientific name *Botia macracanthus*

Subfamily Botiinae

Family Cobitidae

Order Cypriniformes

Size Up to 16 in (40 cm); most specimens attain a size of around 12 in (30 cm)

Key features Pointed, scaleless head with subterminal mouth bearing 2 pairs of rostral barbels; 1 erectile spine under each eye; body compressed; fins well formed, especially caudal fin; adipose fin absent; coloration: orange base color with 3 broad black bands, the first of which passes from top of head through eye and cheeks to "chin" area; second broader—anterior edge starting immediately behind first band and posterior just in front of dorsal fin, this band narrows as it extends downward to end behind pectoral fins; third band covers most of dorsal fin and back, narrowing and extending through anal fin

Breeding Very little known about breeding habits; upriver migrations occur just prior to high-water season; spawning occurs in fast-flowing stretches of rivers; eggs probably hidden under rocks or scattered among crevices; no parental care occurs

Diet Feeds predominantly on bottom-dwelling invertebrates, including (particularly) worms and crustaceans; also takes some plant matter

Habitat Flowing rivers in Kalimantan (Borneo) and Sumatra (Indonesia); in Kalimantan species normally found in brown- or black-water rivers with few suspended sediments; in Sumatra tends to be found in turbid waters; substrate usually contains rocks, pebbles, and sandy areas

Distribution Kalimantan and Sumatra; also introduced into Thailand and Philippines, but these introductions may not have become established

Status Not threatened

Weather Loach

Common name Weather loach (European weather loach, pond loach, weather fish)

Scientific name *Misgurnus fossilis*

Subfamily Cobitinae

Family Cobitidae

Order Cypriniformes

Size Up to a maximum of nearly 14 in (35 cm) but usually a little smaller

Key features Elongated, eel-like body; smallish head with underslung mouth; 5 pairs of barbels; smallish eyes located high on side of head; erectile spine under each eye; sightly rounded dorsal and caudal fins; small anal fin; adipose fin absent; body covered in thick slime; dull light-brown coloration with several dark bands extending from behind head to base of caudal fin

Breeding Spawning from April to June among plants in shallow water; egg laying may extend over several weeks with as many as 170,000 eggs reported (although much smaller spawns are more common); hatching 8–10 days; newly hatched larvae have small, ribbonlike external gills that help them breathe in oxygen-poor waters into which they are frequently born

Diet Bottom-living invertebrates, including worms, mollusks, and insect larvae; some plant material may also be eaten; mainly active from dusk; inactive in daytime except when atmospheric pressure drops, as when storm approaching, at which time becomes hyperactive

Habitat Mainly lowland still waters like floodplains, backwaters, ponds, and marshes—areas that may have fine-grained bottoms with low levels of oxygen, and that may dry up; usually these habitats also heavily vegetated

Distribution Widely distributed in Europe from France, Denmark, and Holland as far eastward as Caspian Sea; absent from southern areas, British Isles, and Scandinavia

Status Not threatened

Headstanders

The 4.7-inch (12-cm) striped headstander (*Anostomus anostomus*) lives in the Amazon and Orinoco basins. It is usually found head-down in well-oxygenated waters. It is a member of the subfamily Anostominae.

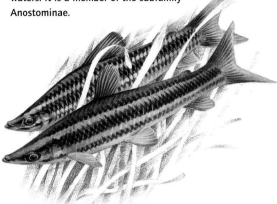

Common name Headstanders

Subfamilies Anostominae, Chilodontinae

Family Anostomidae

Order Characiformes

Number of species Anostominae: 128 in 10 genera; Chilodontinae: 5 in 2 genera

Size From 3.2 in (8 cm) to 16 in (40 cm)

Key features Most species have elongated body, cylindrical in cross-section; notable exceptions: high-backed headstander (*Abramites hypselonotus*) and spotted headstander (*Chilodus punctatus*); head with extended snout ending in small mouth, often with fleshy modifications; in leporins (*Leporinus* spp.) the teeth and lip arrangement creates a "hare-lip" effect; mouth upturned in some species, e.g., members of genus *Anostomus*; eyes large; fins well formed; adipose fin present in all species; body patterns include vertical bands, spots, and longitudinal bands

Breeding Information lacking; spawning migrations upriver may occur; eggs scattered, often among vegetation, and abandoned; hatching takes several days

Diet Plants, including algae; some species feed on insects and other invertebrates

Habitat Variety of waters with medium to strong current; vegetation is often preferred; rocks and clefts are headstander habitats, as well as "blackwater"

Distribution Widely in tropical South America

Status Not threatened

Freshwater Hatchetfish

The marbled hatchetfish (*Carnegiella strigata*) occurs in the Guyanas and Amazon River basin. Although a few other fish species can glide out of water, only hatchetfish use propulsive force to move through the air. Length to 1.4 inches (3.5 cm).

Common name Freshwater hatchetfish

Family Gasteropelecidae

Order Characiformes

Number of species 9 in 3 genera

Size From 1 in (2.5 cm) to 3.2 in (8 cm); aquarium-reared specimens slightly larger

Key features Body with pronounced chest enlargement and keel; head with flat top, upwardly directed mouth; large eyes; dorsal profile straight to dorsal fin; all fins well developed; pectoral fins extremely large and winglike—when confronted by predators it can leap from water and fly a short distance by flapping them; all species have silvery scales on side of body; several species have dark central body line extending to caudal peduncle

Breeding Eggs scattered among roots of floating plants and among vegetation and then abandoned; hatching takes 1.5 days

Diet Lives most of the time just beneath the water surface and picks off insects that fall in; also eats aquatic invertebrates

Habitat *Carnegiella* in small streams and creeks; *Gasteropelecus* and *Thoracocharax* in open waters

Distribution Panama in Central America; South American countries except Chile

Status Not threatened

African Tetras

At 4.5 ft (1.3 m) in length and weighing 110 pounds (50 kg) the tigerfish (*Hydrocynus goliath*) is the biggest member of the family Alestidae. This large, streamlined fish with fanglike teeth is a voracious predator of the Zaire River.

Common name African tetras

Family Alestidae

Order Characiformes

Number of species Around 110 in 18 genera

Size From 0.8 in (2 cm) to 4.5 ft (1.3 m); most within range of 2–4 in (5–10 cm)

Key features Body elongate and compressed, some species with hump behind head and deeper body, e.g., African moonfish (*Bathyaethiops caudomaculatus*); mouth armed with pointed teeth; fins well formed; forked caudal fin in all species; coloration variable, usually includes bright silvery sides to body; many possess black blotch or streak on caudal peduncle

Breeding Spawning late spring to early fall; eggs scattered over bottom and abandoned; hatching from 15 hours to 6–7 days, e.g., eggs of tigerfish (*Hydrocynus goliath*) hatch in 15–22 hours, while Congo tetra (*Phenacogrammus interruptus*) eggs take 6 days or more

Diet Predatory; larger species feed on other fish; smaller ones on insects and other aquatic invertebrates; plant material also eaten

Habitat Fresh waters from streams and pools to large lakes, e.g., Lakes Chad, Albert, Turkana, and Malawi

Distribution Tropical Africa

Status Not threatened

Predator Tetras and S. American Darters

The sailfin tetra (*Crenuchus spilurus*) of Guyana and the middle Amazon region grows to a length of about 2.5 inches (6 cm). Males (shown here) have larger dorsal fins than females.

Common name Predator tetras and South American darters

Subfamilies Crenuchinae (predator tetras and sailfin tetra), Characidiinae (darters)

Family Crenuchidae

Order Characiformes

Number of species Crenuchinae: 3 in 2 genera; Characidiinae: around 74 in 9 genera

Size From 1.2 in (3 cm) to about 4 in (10 cm)

Key features Two distinct body forms: Crenuchinae have large mouths and (in males) large dorsal and anal fins; eyes large; head large; predator tetras have no adipose fin; body compressed; fins well formed; coloration: golden line running the length of body; large black spot on caudal peduncle and red edges to fins in males; fins are also heavily spotted in creamy yellow; predator tetra (*Poecilocharax weitzmani*) vividly marked with colored lines and spots; sides of body have scattered luminous green scales; Characidiinae have long, slim bodies and lack extra-large mouth of Crenuchinae; coloration generally drab with mottled or banded patterns in shades of brown; sides may be whitish or creamish

Breeding Detail lacking; eggs of sailfin tetra (*Crenuchus spilurus*) laid on a stone and fanned by male; darters scatter eggs over substrate and abandon; hatching about 2 days

Diet Insects and invertebrates; larger species eat smaller fish

Habitat Small streams with fast-flowing water, some darter tetras live in fast-flowing rapids and falls, often clinging to bottom rocks or vegetation

Distribution Tropical and subtropical South America from eastern Panama to La Plata in Argentina

Status Not threatened

Piranhas, Silver Dollars, and Pacus

The fearsome red-bellied piranha (*Pygocentrus nattereri*) of the Amazon and Orinoco basins grows up to 12 inches (30 cm) in length.

Common name Piranhas, silver dollars, and pacus

Subfamily Serrasalminae

Family Characidae

Order Characiformes

Number of species About 60 in 13 genera

Size From 6 in (15 cm) to 40 in (1 m)

Key features Body deep and compressed—pronounced in silver dollars; head blunt and massive; lower jaw protruding; sharp cutting teeth in piranhas, grinding teeth in nut and seed-eaters; fins well formed; coloration variable, from shiny and silvery to dull in the pacus and piranhas; some species attractively colored in chest area; fins may be distinctively colored

Breeding Several hundred or even thousand eggs from onset of wet season scattered or laid in prepared site; may or may not be guarded; spawning in pairs or shoals; hatching takes less than 1 week

Diet True piranhas feed on fish and other prey animals (reptiles, birds, and mammals), fruits, and seeds; silver dollars eat quantities of leaves; pacus mainly eat fruits and seeds; a few are specialized fin and scale eaters

Habitat From streams and clear water or blackwater rivers to turbid rivers, lakes, and flooded forests

Distribution Widespread in tropical South America

Status Not threatened

North American Freshwater Catfish

The channel catfish (*Ictalurus punctatus*) lives in rivers, large creeks, ponds, and reservoirs mainly in southern Canada and the east-central United States, although it has been introduced elsewhere. It is a popular sport and food fish. Length to 52 inches (1.3 m).

Common name North American freshwater catfish

Family Ictaluridae

Order Siluriformes

Number of species Around 45 in 7 genera

Size From 4 in (10 cm) long in madtoms and stonecat (*Noturus* spp.) to 19–65 in (48–165 cm) long in channel catfish (*Ictalurus* spp.)

Key features Body moderately elongated and scaleless; 4 pairs of barbels; teeth "velvety" pads (except toothless blindcat, *Trogloglanis pattersoni*—no teeth); stout spine at front of dorsal fin (except in *Prietella*); tail straight or round to moderately forked; adipose fin small and well separated from caudal in most species; in madtoms and stonecat it is long, low, and either joined or almost joined to caudal; madtoms and stonecat can produce venom; all species except widemouth blindcat (*Satan eurystomus*) and toothless blindcat have swim bladders; blindcats have no eyes

Breeding Nests saucer-shaped depressions or scrapings under overhangs, among vegetation, or in cavities; built by one or both spawners and vigorously defended; eggs: as few as 15 in madtoms and up to 10,000 in larger species; guarded by male, but female may play a role; hatching from 5–14 days depending on species and water temperature

Diet Aquatic invertebrates and other small fish; carrion may be taken

Habitat Rivers and lakes with sandy or muddy bottoms; some madtoms prefer fast-flowing waters; blind species prefer artesian wells

Distribution North and Central America from Hudson Bay and St. Lawrence drainages in Canada southward to the Rio Ucumacinta in Guatemala

Status IUCN lists 18 species under various levels of threat

Walking Catfish

The walking catfish (*Clarias batrachus*) is the best-known member of its family. It is found from India to Indonesia, but has also been introduced elsewhere. Length to 18.5 inches (47 cm).

Common name Walking catfish

Family Clariidae

Order Siluriformes

Number of species 100 in around 13 genera

Size From 4.7 in (12 cm) to around 4.6 ft (1.4 m)

Key features Elongated body, with some species eel-like; dorsal and anal fins long-based and lack a spine at the front— these fins may be joined to the caudal fin or may be separate; adipose fin usually absent; pectoral fins usually have spine (used in walking), but both pectoral and pelvic fins may be absent; body scaleless; head often flattened and covered in bony plates; eyes range from well formed to tiny or absent; mouth terminal (located at the tip of the snout) with 4 pairs of long barbels in most species (3 in some); modified gills and arborescent and superbranchial organs present in most genera to allow fish to breathe out of water

Breeding Usually at night, at beginning of rainy season, in shallow water; nesting possible but the eggs left unprotected once spawning completed; hatching around 23–30 hours

Diet From small aquatic insects and other invertebrates to fish and small birds

Habitat A wide range of freshwater habitats including lakes, pools, and backwaters; some live in caves or wells

Distribution Widely in Africa, parts of the Middle East, and southern and western Asia; as a food or aquarium fish in other regions—for example, Florida and Hawaii

Status IUCN lists 8 species under various levels of threat, including cave catfish (*Clarias cavernicola*), *C. maclareni*, *Encheloclarius curtisoma*, and *E. keliodes* as Critically Endangered

Electric Catfish

The electric catfish (*Malapterurus electricus*), a fierce 4-ft (1.2-m) predator widespread in tropical Africa. The electricity it produces is not only used to stun prey and deter predators but also to navigate and detect prey.

Common name Electric catfish

Family Malapteruridae

Order Siluriformes

Number of species 11 in 1 genus (*Malapterurus*)

Size From around 4.8 in (12.2 cm) to around 48 in (1.2 m)

Key features Sturdy head; small eyes; fleshy lips; 3 pairs of mouth barbels; nasal or "nose" barbels lacking; no dorsal fin; adipose fin well formed and located near the tail; rounded caudal fin; different degrees and intensity of mottling and body banding; electricity-producing organ beneath skin located from behind the head to just in front of adipose and anal fins; consists of specialized cells called electrocytes stacked on top of each other

Breeding May spawn in burrows excavated in river banks

Diet Smaller fish

Habitat Slow-moving or still waters containing rocks, sunken logs, and roots where the fish can shelter or rest in daylight hours; many preferred waters are tannin-stained (known as blackwaters) or turbid in nature

Distribution Widespread in tropical Africa from western Africa through central regions to the Nile River; individual species may have restricted ranges

Status Not threatened

Upside-Down Catfish

The 4-inch (10-cm) upside-down catfish (*Synodontis nigriventris*) swims upside down to graze the underside of leaves for algae and tiny animals.

Common name Upside-down catfish (squeakers, squeaking catfish)

Family Mochokidae

Order Siluriformes

Number of species Around 170 in 10 genera

Size From around 2 in (5 cm) to around 27.5 in (70 cm)

Key features Normal-headed species have sloping forehead and slightly to moderately pointed snout; mouth on underside of tip of snout; in sucker-mouthed species mouth is broader and more straight-edged with fleshy lips and broad tooth pads; stout cephalic (head) shield found in all, extending to front of dorsal fin along the top and to the base of pectoral fins along the sides and bottom; 3 pairs of barbels (no nasal barbels), ornate in some; dorsal and pectoral fins possess a stout spine at front, can be "locked" in defense; adipose fin large, becoming sail like in normal-headed species

Breeding Few details available; eggs said to be adhesive and laid under cover; no parental care reported; hatching takes about 1 week; at least 2 species lay eggs among those laid by breeding mouthbrooding cichlids

Diet Small organisms, crustaceans, and plankton; algae scraped off rocks, logs, and submerged vegetation; larger species take small fish

Habitat Prefer slow-moving waters, lakes, and swamps; sucker-mouthed species prefer faster-flowing waters, some in torrents; many spend day hiding under submerged logs and roots or in caves and crevices

Distribution Widespread in most tropical regions of Africa including African Rift lakes

Status IUCN lists Incomati rock catlet (*Chiloglanis bifurcus*) as Critically Endangered

Pikes and Pickerels

At 6 feet (1.8 m) in length, the muskellunge (*Esox masquinongy*) is the longest member of the family Esocidae. This huge North American freshwater predator feeds on a variety of other animals, including fish, ducklings, aquatic mammals such as muskrats, and snakes.

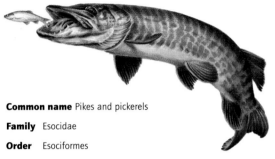

Common name Pikes and pickerels

Family Esocidae

Order Esociformes

Number of species 5 in 1 genus (*Esox*)

Size From around 15.5 in (39.5 cm) to about 6 ft (1.8 m)

Key features Elongated body; large, pointed head with distinct duck-billed snout; large mouth with numerous pointed teeth; lower jaw slightly longer than upper; eyes in top half of head; all fins well formed; no adipose fin; pectoral fins close to gill openings; dorsal and anal fins set well back along body; caudal fin forked; body often mottled with irregular streaks; pale belly

Breeding Usually in spring; males arrive at breeding sites before females; cool, shallow waters preferred, underwater vegetation essential; spawning can occur in groups of 1 female and 2 or 3 males; eggs and sperm scattered among vegetation and spread out over several weeks; large female can release up to 600,000 sticky eggs; no parental protection; hatching takes a few days to nearly a month depending on water temperature

Diet Small fish, insects, and other invertebrates during juvenile stages; larger pikes eat amphibians, larger fish, crayfish, small mammals, waterfowl

Habitat Predominantly fresh water but also in brackish conditions; slow-flowing or still waters preferred, especially heavily vegetated and shallow; can be found at 100 ft (30 m); cool water temperatures preferred but not restricted to such conditions

Distribution Widely distributed in Northern Hemisphere but not naturally occurring in northern Norway or northern Scotland

Status Not threatened

Graylings

The 24-inch (61-cm) European grayling (*Thymallus thymallus*) occurs in Britain and France east to the Ural Mountains in northwest Russia. It inhabits well-oxygenated waters and feeds on insects, nymphs, small worms, and crustaceans.

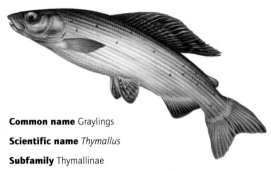

Common name Graylings

Scientific name *Thymallus*

Subfamily Thymallinae

Family Salmonidae

Order Salmoniformes

Number of species 5 (with 1 containing 4 subspecies) in 1 genus

Size From around 7.9 in (20 cm) to about 30 cm (76 cm)

Key features Elongated body, slightly compressed, with deepest point around the "shoulder"; small, sloping head, pointed snout; mouth small and slightly below tip of snout; numerous small teeth on both jaws; medium to largish eyes on top half of head; all fins well formed; dorsal fin sail-like, especially in males, front edge about halfway between line of pectoral and pelvic fins; anal fin set well back in line with adipose fin; caudal fin large and distinctly forked; scales moderately large; dark color on back, fading to silvery along sides and belly; numerous dark spots on body and dorsal fin; color more vivid in males

Breeding In spring female excavates shallow depression (redd) usually in shallow water with sandy or gravelly bottom; male wraps dorsal fin over female's back during spawning; 8,000 or more eggs are buried, hatching out after 3–4 weeks

Diet Mainly bottom-living invertebrates; also feeds from surface, taking flying insects that fall into the water

Habitat Flowing, middle reaches of rivers—the "Grayling Zone"; clear, well-oxygenated water with gravelly or sandy bottom, or riffles between pools

Distribution Widely distributed in Northern Hemisphere; narrower distribution in some species

Status Not threatened

Char

The 34-inch (86-cm) brook char (*Salvelinus fontinalis*) occurs widely in clear, cool, well-oxygenated creeks, small to medium rivers, and lakes in eastern parts of North America.

Common name Char

Scientific names *Salvelinus, Salvethymus*

Subfamily Salmoninae

Family Salmonidae

Order Salmoniformes

Number of species 39 in 2 genera

Size From around 9.5 in (24 cm) to around 4.9 ft (1.5 m)

Key features Streamlined body; rounded to pointed snout with rounded tip; large mouth; teeth on both jaws; eyes moderate to large; all fins well formed; dorsal has fewer than 16 rays, lacks spines; adipose fin present; caudal fin slightly forked or almost straight-edged; anal fin set well back on body; pelvic fins on belly; pectoral fins behind and below gill covers; minute scales; variable coloration; typical spotted body; dark back and top of sides, lighter lower sides and belly; white front edge on anal and pelvic fins

Breeding Anadromous species and populations migrate from the sea into rivers to spawn; landlocked (lake-dwelling) species and populations migrate into nearby rivers or remain in lake to search out gravelly areas; males establish territories, which females enter to excavate shallow depression (redd); pair release eggs and sperm in the redd; eggs take up to 70 days to hatch; adults return to sea or lake after spawning

Diet Invertebrates from plankton, sponges, worms, and crustaceans to aquatic and terrestrial insects; also fish, amphibians, and small mammals

Habitat Some species spend most of year at sea; migrate into fresh water to spawn; landlocked species in cool, flowing stretches, pools, and lakes

Distribution Northern Hemisphere; some species wide-ranging, others restricted

Status IUCN lists 1 species as Endangered, 2 (including *Salvethymus*) Vulnerable, 1 Extinct

Huchen or Danube Salmon

Common name Huchen or Danube salmon (hunchen, European river trout, Danube trout)

Scientific name *Hucho hucho*

Subfamily Salmoninae

Family Salmonidae

Order Salmoniformes

Size Around 4.9 ft (1.5 m) but reported up to 6.5 ft (2 m)

Key features Elongated, cigar-shaped body; large head; broad mouth with numerous teeth; back edge extends beyond eye; eyes close to top of head; all fins well formed; dorsal fin in front of pelvic fins; anal fin set well back along body in line with adipose fin; powerful forked tail; scales very small; dark greenish on back, silvery sides with a pink sheen, white belly; numerous small X-shaped dark spots on body

Breeding Early to midspring over gravelly beds in fast-flowing water; female excavates shallow depression (redd), in which she lays and buries her eggs; hatching takes up to 5 weeks; no parental protection

Diet Juveniles feed on invertebrates; adults feed almost exclusively on fish; also amphibians, reptiles, mammals, and waterfowl

Habitat Prefers tributaries of large, well-oxygenated, fast-flowing rivers but also found in backwaters

Distribution Native to the Danube River basin

Status Listed by IUCN as Endangered mainly due to pollution, overfishing, draining of habitat, damming of rivers, and excessive removal of water for industry and agriculture

Atlantic Salmon

Sockeye Salmon

Common name Atlantic salmon (salmon and many other names)

Scientific name *Salmo salar*

Subfamily Salmoninae

Family Salmonidae

Order Salmoniformes

Size Extremely variable at maturity but up to 4.9 ft (1.5 m)

Key features Elongated body; pointed snout with rounded tip; large mouth; numerous teeth in both jaws; dorsal fin slightly in front of pelvic fin line; adipose fin present; tail slightly forked; anal fin slightly in front of adipose fin line; pelvic fins on belly; scales very small; fish returning from sea predominantly silver with darker back and white belly; pectoral fins relatively low and behind gill covers; sides have small, X-shaped spots; male's jaw becomes hooked (a kype)

Breeding In fresh water usually between October and January in flowing streams with gravelly bottoms; female excavates nests (redds); eggs covered, then abandoned; adults return to sea or home lake; most oceangoing adults die before entering sea, but some (mostly females) survive; eggs hatch after several months

Diet Young fish eat plankton and small invertebrates, then larger invertebrates; oceangoing adults' diet is squid, shrimp, and fish; landlocked adults eat freshwater crustaceans and fish

Habitat Open sea close to coasts during prespawning phase in migrating populations; deep pools and river stretches in landlocked populations; clear, oxygen-rich, flowing waters preferred by latter; same conditions required for spawning; shallow water preferred by all populations

Distribution Both sides of northern Atlantic Ocean; in the west from northern Quebec in Canada to Connecticut; in the east from Arctic Circle to Portugal, southern Greenland and Iceland to Barents Sea; introduced into many locations, including Australia, New Zealand, Argentina, Chile; some introductions not established

Status Not threatened

Common name Sockeye salmon (red salmon, kokanee, and many others)

Scientific name *Oncorhynchus nerka*

Subfamily Salmoninae

Family Salmonidae

Order Salmoniformes

Size Wide range of sizes at maturity: from around 16 in (40 cm) to about 33 in (84 cm)

Key features Elongated body; moderately pointed snout with rounded tip; large mouth extending beyond eye in large specimens; teeth on both jaws; eyes relatively small; all fins well formed; back edge of dorsal fin in line with front edge of pelvic fins; adipose fin present; tail slightly forked; anal fin in front of line of adipose fin; pelvic fins on belly; pectoral fins behind and below gill covers; tiny scales; sea-based stocks are blue-black along back with silvery belly; small black specks along back and caudal fin; body becomes brilliant red during breeding season in both males and females; fins (except caudal and pectorals) also become red, head becomes green; male's jaw develops into a pronounced hook (kype) during breeding season

Breeding Fresh water: shallow, flowing, oxygen-rich streams with gravelly bottoms; some spawn along lake or island shores at depths of 7–10 ft (2.3 m), occasionally down to 100 ft (30 m); female excavates redd; female covers eggs as she digs a new redd at front edge of the one in which she has laid her eggs; all adults die after spawning; hatching takes 6 weeks to 5 months; landlocked stocks (kokanee) remain in fresh water

Diet Young fish eat plankton, then small fish and larger invertebrates; sockeye eat larger fish during oceangoing stages; kokanee eat invertebrates

Habitat Mature in open sea at depths of up to 820 ft (250 m); landlocked populations in lakes

Distribution Both coasts of Pacific; in the east from Alaska down to California; in the west around Japan and Russia; introduced to several countries

Status Not threatened

Sea, Brown, Brook, Lake Trout

Common name Sea, brown, brook, lake trout

Scientific name *Salmo trutta*

Subfamily Salmoninae

Family Salmonidae

Order Salmoniformes

Size From about 9.4 in (24 cm) to about 4.6 ft (1.4 m)

Key features Elongated body; pointed snout with rounded to blunt tip; large mouth, upper jaw extending beyond eye; dorsal fin in front of line of pelvic fins; adipose fin present; tail almost straight-edged; anal fin almost in line with adipose fin; pelvic fins on belly, closer to anal than pectoral fins; pectoral fins right behind and below gill covers; variable coloration: estuary and sea-living populations have few dark body spots; freshwater populations heavily spotted; almost black or brown along back, fading to orange down sides and yellowish or whitish along belly; body spots predominantly very dark with fewer rusty-red spots

Breeding In fresh water usually between October and January; no large-scale migration; most adults survive breeding season to spawn again

Diet Mostly aquatic insects, crustaceans, and aerial insects; larger specimens eat fish, plus snails, tadpoles, frogs, toads, newts, and salamanders

Habitat Sea trout (*Salmo trutta trutta*), brown trout (*S. t. fario*), and *S. t. macrostigma* spend time at sea, return to fresh water to spawn; Aral trout (*S. t. aralensis*), Amu-Darya trout (*S. t. oxianus*), and lake trout (*S. t. lacustris*) restricted to fresh water; well-oxygenated, clear, flowing waters preferred by all types; sea trout remain in top 33 ft (10 m), *S. t. macrostigma* descend to depths of 3,300–8,200 ft (1,000–2,500 m); in rivers and lakes, preferring sheltered locations in shallow, flowing water

Distribution Eurasia; also introduced into many countries

Status IUCN lists Aral trout as Critically Endangered

Rainbow Trout

Common name Rainbow trout (steelhead, plus many others)

Scientific name *Oncorhynchus mykiss*

Subfamily Salmoninae

Family Salmonidae

Order Salmoniformes

Size Nearly 4 ft (1.2 m) maximum; some populations, especially some landlocked ones, smaller and lighter

Key features Elongated body; pointed snout with rounded to blunt tip; large mouth, upper jaw extending beyond eye in large specimens; teeth in both jaws; older males have hooked lower jaw; dorsal fin almost in line with pelvic fins; adipose fin present; tail slightly forked; back edge of anal fin almost in line with adipose fin; pelvic fins on belly, closer to anal than to pectoral fins; pectoral fins immediately behind and below gill covers; variable coloration: steelheads steel-gray and silvery during oceangoing phase, changing to rainbow coloring in fresh water; pinkish "rainbow" band runs from cheeks to caudal peduncle; numerous black spots along bluish-black back and down sides

Breeding Behavior like other trout and salmon; breeding season largely depends on location; egg laying occurs during December in south, as late as May or June in far north; eggs hatch after 1 month depending on temperature

Diet Wide range of aquatic invertebrates and aerial insects; larger specimens also take fish

Habitat Landlocked and other exclusively freshwater populations (rainbows) tolerate conditions from fast-flowing, oxygen-rich streams to still lakes; oceangoing populations (steelheads) travel hundreds of miles out to sea but remain in top 655 ft (209 m) of water column

Distribution Natural range: eastern Pacific coast of North America from Alaska southward to parts of Mexico; introduced into numerous countries

Status Not threatened

Barbeled Dragonfish

The 9.5-inch (24-cm) stoplight loosejaw (*Malacosteus niger*) occurs at depths down to 8,200 feet (2,500 m) in the Atlantic (from Greenland to Scotland), Indian (from the Gulf of Aden to the Bay of Bengal), and Pacific Oceans (China, Australia, and New Zealand east to South America and north to British Columbia).

Common name Barbeled dragonfish

Family Stomiidae

Subfamilies Astronesthinae (snaggletooths), Stomiinae (scaly dragonfish), Chauliodontinae (viperfish), Melanostomiinae (scaleless black dragonfish), Idiacanthinae (black dragonfish), Malacosteinae (loosejaws)

Order Stomiiformes

Number of species Around 278 in some 27 genera

Size From about 1 in (2.5 cm) to about 20 in (50 cm)

Key features Elongated to very elongated body; body naked except in 2 species that may have scales or scalelike markings plus a jellylike covering; chin barbel present in most species; mouth typically large; numerous fanglike teeth, very long in many species; adipose fin absent in most subfamilies; snaggletooths and viperfish have an additional adipose fin in front of anal fin; all species have photophores, usually in large numbers, mainly along lower half of body and belly; also photophores at tip of chin barbel and on cheeks in many species; majority are dark-colored, many are black

Breeding Breeding and mating behavior unknown; eggs and larvae planktonic; larvae often quite different than adult; most extreme differences found in black dragonfish, whose males and females are also different

Diet Crustaceans and fish; large prey taken even by modest-sized individuals

Habitat Daily migrations made by many species, rising to shallower depths during night; adults of some species occur at or near surface during hours of darkness, descending to depths in excess of 9,850 ft (3,000 m)

Distribution Atlantic, Indian, and Pacific Oceans

Status Not threatened

Marine Hatchetfish

The 3.3-inch (8.4-cm) Pacific hatchetfish (*Argyropelecus affinis*) occurs in the Atlantic from the Gulf of Mexico east to the Gulf of Guinea, as well as the Indian and Pacific Oceans. It is mainly found between 985 and 2,130 feet (300–650 m), but it can go as deep as 12,700 feet (3,870 m).

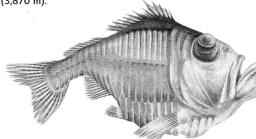

Common name Marine hatchetfish (pearlsides, constellationfish, and allies)

Family Sternoptychidae

Subfamilies Maurolicinae (pearlsides and constellationfish); Sternoptychinae (marine hatchetfish)

Order Stomiiformes

Number of species About 71 in 10 genera

Size From around 0.8 in (2 cm) to 5.5 in (14 cm)

Key features Maurolicinae: elongated body, never compressed; mouth directed at upward angle; eyes almost central on head in normal direction or above center and directed upward; Sternoptychinae: deep, extremely compressed body; mouth directed nearly vertically; eyes in top half of head, directed upward, telescopic in some species; keel-like chest; bladelike structure formed from pterygiophores in front of dorsal fin; rear of body slim (the hatchet "handle"); all speces have photophores (light-producing organs), some inside mouth

Breeding Unknown for most species, but eggs and larvae planktonic; pearlsides (*Maurolicus* spp.) mature in 1 year, spawn March to September, producing 200–500 eggs; constellationfish (*Valenciennellus tripunctulatus*) may only live for 1 year but spawn many times, producing 100–360 eggs each time

Diet Predominantly invertebrates, including copepods; some species also eat small fish

Habitat Most are deepwater species though not living on the bottom; depth ranges from the surface down to more than 12,000 ft (3,660 m); many hatchetfish never rise above 650 ft (200 m), some remain in deeper water at 1,300 ft (400 m)

Distribution Atlantic, Indian, and Pacific Oceans

Status Not threatened

Lizardfish

The 12.5-inch (32-cm) gracile lizardfish (*Saurida gracilis*) occurs in shallow lagoons and coral reefs in the Indo-Pacific from the Red Sea and East Africa to the Great Barrier Reef north to Hawaii and Japan. This active predator feeds on fish at night.

Common name Lizardfish

Family Synodontidae

Subfamilies Synodontinae (lizardfish), Harpadontinae (Bombay duck), Bathysaurinae

Order Aulopiformes

Number of species About 64 in 5 genera

Size From 3.5 in (9 cm) to around 30 in (78 m)

Key features Elongated body with large, toothed mouth in all species; eyes large in all, but Bombay ducks have very small eyes; all fins well formed, adipose fin may be absent in Bathysaurinae and some lizardfish; scales over whole body but confined to lateral line and posterior half of body in Bombay ducks; lateral line scales enlarged in Bathysaurinae; variable colors, often mottled

Breeding Eggs and sperm are scattered, then abandoned; sexes separate in all but two species, which are synchronous hermaphrodites (both male and female at same time)—deep-sea lizardfish (*Bathysaurus ferox*) and highfin lizardfish (*B. mollis*)

Diet Fish and invertebrates, primarily crustaceans

Habitat Relatively shallow water like coral reefs and rocky or sandy bottoms; Bathysaurinae occur in deeper, colder waters at depths of 15,750 ft (4,800 m) for 1 species; Bombay ducks enter estuaries, swimming upriver in prebreeding migrations; Synodontinae spend much of their time sitting on the bottom or buried in the substratum with just their eyes showing

Distribution Atlantic, Indian, and Pacific Oceans

Status Not threatened

Crestfish

The 6.5-foot (2-m) crested oarfish (*Lophotus lacepede*) occurs in warmer waters of both the Atlantic and the Pacific, feeding on anchovies and squid.

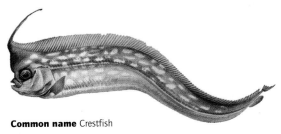

Common name Crestfish

Family Lophotidae

Order Lampridiformes

Number of species 3 in 2 genera

Size From around 4.9 ft (1.5 m) to 6.5 ft (2 m)

Key features Extremely elongated, ribbonlike body; head blunt but with projecting forehead extended into a long, horizontal, hornlike structure in the unicorn crestfish (*Eumecichthys fiski*); mouth extremely extendable; eyes large; dorsal fin originates at tip of forehead and extends to tail; caudal fin small; anal fin very small, positioned close to tail; pelvic fins usually absent; adipose fin absent; small pectoral fins located close to gill covers; scales absent or small and easily dislodged, giving scaleless appearance; silvery base with dark vertical bands in unicorn crestfish, speckling in other 2 species; fins red in all 3 species; when alarmed or needing to make a quick escape, can produce black or dark-brown inklike substance from special organ close to the gut

Breeding Behavior unknown; eggs and larvae are planktonic; eggs of crested oarfish (*Lophotus lacepede*) covered in amber-colored spines

Diet Mainly fish, squid, and other invertebrates

Habitat Open-water species sometimes found close to surface or at depths exceeding 3,300 ft (1,000 m)

Distribution Found in most oceans

Status Not threatened

Ribbonfish

The 9.8-foot (3-m) peregrine ribbonfish (*Trachipterus trachypterus*) occurs at depths down to 1,640 feet (500 m) in the eastern Atlantic from the Mediterranean to South Africa and in the Pacific from Japan south to New Zealand and Chile. It swims with its head up and feeds on squid and midwater fish.

Common name Ribbonfish (dealfish)

Family Trachipteridae

Order Lampridiformes

Number of species 10 in 3 genera (*Desmodema, Trachipterus, Zu*)

Size From 3.6 ft (1.1 m) to 9.8 ft (3 m)

Key features Elongated body tapers to varying degrees; head usually large; snout either steeply sloping or pointed; large mouth and eyes; dorsal fin extends from head to tail, first few rays generally extended; tail large or small, either with just the upper lobe present or (additionally) with much-reduced lower lobe rays; tail at sharp angle to body, often perpendicular; anal and adipose fins absent; pelvic fins have very few rays (even just 1) or absent; pectoral fins directly behind gill covers; body naked (scales are easily dislodged); usually silvery, sometimes speckled; some species: distinctive spots along back

Breeding Behavior unknown; eggs and larvae planktonic; egg surface frequently with irregularities such as tiny "pits"; larvae look very different than adults, with numerous filamentlike growths that gradually disappear

Diet Fish and squid; also crustaceans

Habitat Open ocean at depths ranging from the surface down to 3,300 ft (1,000 m); some species enter brackish water or found close to shore

Distribution Arctic, Atlantic (into the Mediterranean), Indian, and Pacific Oceans

Status Not threatened

Oarfish

The 36-foot (11-m) oarfish, or king-of-the-herrings (*Regalecus glesne*), occurs in the Atlantic (including the Mediterranean), Indo-Pacific, and Pacific Oceans from southern California to Chile. It lives at great depths between 66 and 3,300 feet (20–1,000 m) and feeds on crustaceans, small fish, and squid.

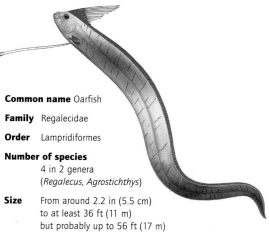

Common name Oarfish

Family Regalecidae

Order Lampridiformes

Number of species 4 in 2 genera (*Regalecus, Agrostichthys*)

Size From around 2.2 in (5.5 cm) to at least 36 ft (11 m) but probably up to 56 ft (17 m)

Key features Elongated, ribbonlike body; blunt head; large extendable mouth; teeth absent; eyes relatively small; dorsal fin with extremely long base originating above eye and extending to tail; front rays extended ending in small flaps; tail also has extended rays; anal and adipose fins absent; pelvic fins extended with long, paddlelike structures and flap at tips; pectoral fins small and located close to gill covers; body scaleless; silvery blue with dark blotches and streaks; reddish fins

Breeding Behavior unknown; spawning occurs during second half of year; larvae bearing extremely long rays on front of dorsal fin have been collected near surface

Diet Mostly free-swimming, small invertebrates, particularly euphasiids (luminescent, shrimplike crustaceans); also squid and small fish

Habitat Open ocean down to at least 3,300 ft (1,000 m); can also occur at relatively shallow depths but in open water; specimens occasionally washed up on beaches

Distribution All oceans, extending into the Mediterranean Sea for 1 species

Status Not threatened

Cavefish

Like other cave-dwelling species in the family, the 4.5-inch (11-cm) northern cavefish (*Amblyopsis spelaea*) eats little, breeds slowly, and moves no more than is necessary. Cavefish are difficult to spook—even if they come unexpectedly into contact with another living thing, they turn calmly to one side and move unhurriedly on their way.

Common name Cavefish (swampfish)

Family Amblyopsidae

Order Percopsiformes

Number of species 6 in 4 genera

Size Up to 5 in (13 cm) long

Key features Pale, spindle-shaped fish; single dorsal and anal fins of similar size, each with 7–12 rays located well back on body; in *Typhlichthys subterraneus* first 1 or 2 rays are spiny; in all other species rays are soft and usually branched near tips; large, soft-rayed, rounded tail fin; most species have only 1 set of paired fins, the pectorals, which are roughly oval; pelvic fins absent in all but northern cavefish (*Amblyopsis spelaea*), in which they are present but very small with 3–5 soft rays; vestigial, nonfunctional eyes in cave-dwelling species; 4 species live exclusively in caves and are typically slow moving

Breeding Little is known, but cave species appear to brood eggs and larvae in gill chambers

Diet Small invertebrates such as insects, spiders, myriapods, and other crustaceans

Habitat Caves, springs, and swamps

Distribution Restricted to limestone regions of southeastern U.S., particularly the Mississippi basin

Status IUCN lists Ozark cavefish (*A. rosae*), the northern cavefish, and *Typhlichthys subterraneus* as Vulnerable; and Alabama cavefish (*Speoplatyrhinus poulsoni*) as Critically Endangered

Cod and Haddock

The Atlantic cod (*Gadus morhua*) can grow to 50 inches (1.3 m). This popular food fish occurs in the North Atlantic from Cape Hatteras to Ungava Bay around Greenland and Iceland east to the Barents Sea and south to the Bay of Biscay. As omnivorous predators, they eat all kinds of marine invertebrates and fish, even young cod.

Common name Cod and haddock

Family Gadidae

Order Gadiformes

Number of species About 30 in 15 genera

Size From 6 to 50 inches (15–130 cm)

Key features Slim, torpedo-shaped body; three dorsal fins; two anal fins; paired pelvic fins in front of pectorals; most species with conspicuous barbel on chin

Breeding Spawn in spring; reach adulthood at 2 to 4 years

Diet Aquatic invertebrates and other fish; sometimes smaller individuals of same or related species; strong, needlelike teeth ideal for grasping slippery, wriggling prey; in species that have chin barbel, it is covered with "tastebuds" and can be used to sample potential food before ingestion

Habitat Demersal and benthopelagic (living close to, but not on, bottom) in marine, brackish, and fresh waters; gregarious, often migratory

Distribution Predominantly a Northern Hemisphere family, in Arctic, Atlantic, and Pacific Oceans and adjoining rivers and seas; greatest numbers congregate where the warm waters of the Gulf Stream collide with cool Arctic currents, creating highly productive zone where their preferred foods are abundant

Status IUCN lists Atlantic cod (*Gadus morhua*) and haddock (*Melanogrammus aeglefinus*) as Vulnerable; of other species some are stable, some Critically Endangered

Toadfish

The 15-inch (38-cm) American oyster toadfish (*Opsanus tau*) is also known as the oyster cracker. This venomous species occurs in the western Atlantic from Massachusetts to the West Indies. Living up to its name, this fish eats oysters, other shellfish, most invertebrates, and smaller fish. It is confined to shallow water.

Common name Toadfish (midshipmen, venomous toadfish)

Family Batrachoididae

Subfamily Batrachoidinae (toadfish), Porichthyinae (midshipmen), Thalassophryninae (venomous toadfish)

Order Batrachoidiformes

Number of species About 69 species in 19 genera

Size Up to 15 in (38 cm) long

Key features Large head; very wide mouth; ribs reduced; pelvic fins jugular with one spine and 2–3 soft rays; nocturnal; usually solitary; highly vocal; venomous toadfish have hollow dorsal spines that can deliver poison into the flesh of a victim, causing tissue damage and severe pain

Breeding In shallow water in spring and summer; males use vocalizations or bioluminescence to attract a mate; males prepare nest in cavity, usually a rock but sometimes in discarded can or other garbage; eggs are large; some species show parental care

Diet Omnivorous but mainly other fish, mollusks, and crustaceans

Habitat Marine; bottom-dwelling; toadfish in shallow water, midshipmen in deeper areas of continental shelf

Distribution Widespread in tropical and temperate seas, but most species restricted to Atlantic and Pacific waters off North and South America

Status IUCN lists 6 species as Vulnerable

Goosefish

The American goosefish (*Lophius americanus*) can reach lengths of over 4 feet (1.2 m). This grim, voracious predator, found at depths of 330 feet (100 m) in the western Atlantic, will eat anything that comes close to its lure, including fish and all kinds of invertebrates.

Common name Goosefish

Family Lophiidae

Order Lophiiformes

Number of species 25 species in 4 genera

Size Up to 4 ft (1.2 m) long

Key features Huge, broad head tapers to dorsoventrally flattened body; enormous mouth lined with many hundreds of teeth; lower jaw fringed with small frills of skin; first dorsal fin modified into mobile fishing lure that can be waved in imitation of a scrap of food while its owner remains invisible, often partially buried; solitary; nocturnal

Breeding Spawning takes place in spring in deep water, when up to 2.5 million eggs are released in a mass of floating jelly; young goosefish have very long ventral fins that gradually shrink as they develop; larvae spend early lives feeding on plankton near the surface and head for seafloor when they reach about 3 in (8 cm) long

Diet Carnivorous; mainly other fish attracted by lure and swallowed whole, but also small sharks, large crabs, and even diving seabirds

Habitat Marine; benthic (bottom-dwelling)

Distribution More or less cosmopolitan; in all major oceans and adjoining seas

Status Not threatened

Frogfish

Deep-Sea Anglerfish

As its name suggests, the 4.5-inch (11-cm) longlure frogfish (*Antennarius multiocellatus*), also known as the flagpole frogfish, has a long dorsal spine modified into a lure for attracting prey. This species occurs down to 200 feet (60 m) in the Atlantic from Bermuda and the Bahamas south to Brazil and east to the Ascension Islands and the Azores. It eats small fish and crustaceans lured close enough to ambush.

Female humpback anglerfish (*Melanocetus johnsonii*), shown here, grow no larger than 7 inches (18 cm), but they dwarf the males, which rarely exceed 1 inch (2.5 cm) in length. The species lives in deep water in tropical and temperate oceans.

Common name Frogfish

Family Antennariidae

Order Lophiiformes

Number of species 43 species in 14 genera

Size From about 1 to 13 in (0.5–33 cm) in length

Key features Body often almost spherical; may be dorsoventrally flattened; paired fins are muscular and armlike; first ray of dorsal fin modified into fishing lure, shape and size of which varies according to species; can change skin color to match surroundings in just a few hours; various strange flaps and frills also help break up the body outline, creating perfect camouflage; solitary; nocturnal

Breeding Fertilized eggs float in gelatinous rafts; young live and feed in plankton community

Diet Carnivorous; catch smaller fish and invertebrates using lure that looks like a small, darting fish when waved around; occasionally cannibalistic

Habitat Marine; most species benthic (bottom-dwelling), although sargassum fish (*Histrio histrio*) live in midwater with dense seaweed growth.

Distribution Widespread in tropical and subtropical oceans and adjoining seas around the world

Status Not threatened

Common name Deep-sea anglerfish

Families Linophrynidae, Caulophrynidae, Neoceratiidae, Melanocetidae, Himantolophidae, Diceratiidae, Oneirodidae, Thaumatichthyidae, Centrophrynidae, Ceratiidae, Gigantactinidae

Order Lophiiformes

Number of species About 174 species in 11 families

Size Most spp. less than 8 in (20 cm) long; largest sea devils up to 40 in (1 m); males always very small

Key features Most with globular body; skin covered in blotches and colored in dull shades of black, brown, or olive-green; head large; mouth often gapes to reveal rows of needle-sharp teeth; lack pelvic fins; fishing lure emanates from fin ray and varies from short stub to elaborate, fleshy growth, usually bioluminescent; solitary

Breeding Dwarf males either free living or parasitic on females; eggs spawned in gelatinous mass; hatch into pelagic larvae

Diet Females carnivorous; prey on other fish and deep-sea invertebrates attracted by fishing lure that contains bioluminescent bacteria to illuminate the tip (known as the esca); free-living males feed on plankton; male parasites share resources via blood connection with female and are unable to survive without her

Habitat Marine; pelagic in deep water

Distribution Tropical and subtropical oceans worldwide

Status Little known because habitat so inaccessible

Ricefish and Allies

The Japanese medaka (*Oryzias latipes*) is a shoaling species about 1.5 inches (4 cm) long. It is distributed in China, South Korea, and Japan, and is reported to be established in Java and Malaysia, as well as having been introduced to many other places.

Common name Ricefish and allies

Family Adrianichthyidae

Order Beloniformes

Number of species Around 25 in 4 genera

Size From 0.8 in (2 cm) to 7 in (18 cm)

Key features Elongated, compressed body; head large; well-formed eyes; mouth directed upward; dorsal profile straight or almost straight; dorsal and anal fins set well back along the body; fins usually well formed; coloration: variable—from translucent in Malabar ricefish (*Horaichthys setnai*) to spotted and grayish with silvery sides in Sarasin's minnow, *Xenopoecilus saranisorum*

Breeding Eggs fertilized internally or externally; female carries batches of fertilized eggs attached to area around genital opening; eggs released among vegetation

Diet Small insects and aquatic invertebrates; larger species take small fish

Habitat Streams, ditches, canals, or ponds, often with dense plant growth, or in brackish water

Distribution India to Japan and on to the Indo-Australian archipelago

Status IUCN lists 10 species as variously threatened, including 3 Endangered and 2 Critically Endangered

Flying Fish, Needlefish, Sauries

The flying fish (*Exocoetus volitans*) is about 12 inches (30 cm) long. It is found in tropical and subtropical regions of all the world's oceans. It is a "two-winged" species, using only the pectoral fins for flight.

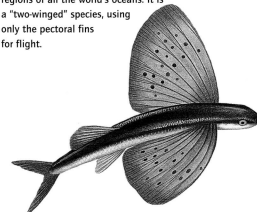

Common name Flying fish, needlefish, and sauries

Families Exocoetidae (flying fish), Belonidae (needlefish), Scomberesocidae (sauries)

Order Beloniformes

Number of species Exocoetidae: 67 in 8 genera; Belonidae: around 45 species in 10 genera; Scomberesocidae: 5 in 3 genera

Size Exocoetidae: from 5.5 in (14 cm) to 20 in (50 cm); Belonidae: from around 1.5 in (4 cm) to 5 ft (1.5 m); Scomberesocidae: from 3 in (7.5 cm) to 20 in (50 cm)

Key features Body elongated; dorsal and anal fins set well back; caudal forked, lobe size varies: in flying fish lower lobe larger than upper with some stiffened rays; in needlefish both lobes similar; in sauries both lobes equal size; pectoral fins large and winglike in flying fish; sauries have series of 5–7 small "fins"; well-formed eyes; flying fish have short jaw; needlefish have beaklike jaws armed with needlelike teeth; sauries may be long beaked or short beaked; coloration: all species deep blue to lighter blue; sides and belly silvery

Breeding Spawning during warmer months in open waters; some needlefish spawn close to coastline; flying fish may spawn among mats of floating seaweeds; all eggs float

Diet Predatory; flying fish feed on plankton; needlefish and sauries feed on smaller fish

Habitat Flying fish and sauries marine; some needlefish marine, but there are 11 freshwater species

Distribution Tropical and temperate regions

Status Not threatened

Topminnows and Killifish

Four-Eyed Fish and Allies

The mummichog (*Fundulus heteroclitus*) is one of several species that is able to live in a variety of different types of habitats, ranging from the sea to fresh water. Length to 6 inches (15 cm).

The four-eyed fish *Anableps anableps* is the best-known species in the family. About 12 inches (30 cm) in length, it is found along coasts, estuaries, and in lakes.

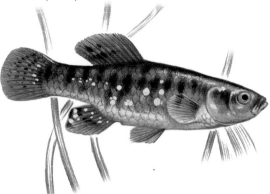

Common name Topminnows and killifish

Family Fundulidae

Order Cyprinodontiformes

Number of species 40 in around 5 genera

Size From 1.4 in (3.5 cm) to 8 in (20 cm); many 3–4 in (7.6–10 cm)

Key features Elongated body; exception is diamond killifish (*Adinia xenica*) with deep body and sharply pointed snout; snout more rounded in most; mouth predominantly directed upward; head flattened; large eyes; dorsal and anal fins set well back; tail fin rounded; coloration variable, often with numerous dark or colored spots on body

Breeding Eggs scattered over a week or longer among vegetation and abandoned; hatching takes several days to over 2 weeks

Diet Small invertebrates including insects

Habitat Freshwater streams and ponds, brackish estuaries and mangrove zones, to coastal stretches and marine lagoons; some, e.g., the mummichog (*Fundulus heteroclitus*) can occupy the whole range

Distribution From Canada southward through North America to the Yucatán (Mexico) and Bermuda and Cuba

Status Not threatened

Common name Four-eyed fish and allies

Family Anablepidae

Order Cyprinodontiformes

Number of species 13 in 3 genera

Size From around 1 in (2.5 cm) to 13.8 in (35 cm)

Key features Four-eyed fish (*Anableps* spp.) elongate; prominent eyes set high on head; mouth under tip of fleshy snout; dorsal profile straight to the tail; dorsal fin set far back; fins well formed; anal fin in males modified into gonopodium. One-sided livebearers (*Jenynsia* spp.) less elongate; eyes on top half of head; blunt snout; dorsal fin farther forward; gonopodium present. White-eye (*Oxyzgonectes dovii*) elongate; snout pointed; eyes large, positioned centrally on side of head; dorsal profile curved; dorsal fin set well back; fins well formed

Breeding In four-eyed fish and one-sided livebearers eggs fertilized internally; female retains eggs and developing embryos; white-eye is egg layer—eggs fertilized externally and abandoned

Diet Vegetation and small invertebrates

Habitat One-sided livebearers fresh water; four-eyed fish in fresh water and brackish water; white-eye in fresh water and brackish water; all species often in open water

Distribution Four-eyed (*A. anableps*) and largescale four-eyed (*A. microlepis*) in South America: Pacific four-eyed fish (*A. dowii*) in Pacific drainages of Central America; one-sided livebearers South America; white-eye in Panama and Costa Rica

Status Not threatened

Guppies, Swordtails, and Lampeyes

The guppy (*Poecilia reticulata*) is a 2-inch (5-cm) fish originally from parts of South America and the West Indies, but now also introduced into other areas. This is a female.

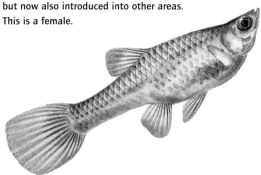

Common name Guppies, swordtails, lampeyes

Family Poeciliidae

Subfamilies Poeciliinae, Fluviphylacinae, Aplocheilichyinae

Order Cyprinodontiformes

Number of species Poeciliinae: around 200 in 20 genera; Fluviphylacinae: 1 species; Aplocheilichyinae: about 100 in around 7 genera

Size From around 0.8 in (2.2 cm) to 8 in (20 cm)

Key features Body shape varies from elongated slim forms with smallish fins to sturdier forms with enlarged fins; upward-directed mouth at tip of snout; eyes large; pectoral fins toward front of belly/chest; in livebearers anal fin is an elongated mating organ; in egg layers anal fin not modified; adipose fin absent; coloration extremely variable

Breeding In livebearers fertilized eggs retained in body until hatching, except in Tommy (*Tomeurus gracilis*); in egg layers eggs scattered among vegetation and abandoned

Diet Invertebrates; some, e.g., piketop livebearer (*Belonesox belizanus*), feed on other fish; also plants, e.g., mollies (some *Poecilia* spp.)

Habitat From shady forest streams to lakes, rivers, estuaries, and coastal waters; most live in surface layers

Distribution Poeciliinae and Fluviphylacinae from Florida to South America; Aplocheilichthyinae in Africa

Status IUCN lists 25 species of livebearer poeciliids as under various levels of threat

Fangtooths and Allies

The 6-inch (15-cm) common fangtooth (*Anoplogaster cornuta*) occurs between 1,640 and 16,400 feet (500–5,000 m). These predators are, in turn, hunted by tuna and marlin.

Common name Fangtooths and allies

Families Anoplogastridae (fangtooths), Anomalopidae (flashlight or lanterneye fish), Monocentridae (pineapple and pinecone fish), Trachichthyidae (roughies, sawbellies, and slimeheads), Holocentridae (squirrelfish and soldierfish)

Order Beryciformes

Number of species Anoplogastridae: 2 in 1 genus; Anomalopidae: 8 in 6 genera; Monocentridae: 4 in 2 genera; Trachichthyidae: around 44 in 8 genera; Holocentridae: around 83 in 8 genera

Size From 2 in (5 cm) to 30 in (75 cm)

Key features Longish to oval body shape; body scales range from very small to large and platelike; head from blunt to more pointed, moderately large to very large; light organ under eye or on lower jaw; eyes relatively large to large in most species (small in fangtooths); powerful fanglike teeth (fangtooths); 1 dorsal fin (spines in front, soft rays in back); pronounced dorsal fin notch (lanternfish) or 2 separate fins (pineapple fish); variable coloration: yellow through red to brown and black; some species have light or dark patterns, luminescence produced inside bodies

Breeding Few details available; eggs and sperm released into water where fertilization takes place; no parental care; eggs take a few weeks to hatch; larvae usually live among plankton for some time

Diet Mainly fish; some invertebrates

Habitat Relatively shallow tropical and subtropical, also temperate, waters; deepwater species (fangtooth) down to 16,400 ft (5,000 m); many in caves or under ledges during day, rise to surface at night.

Distribution Atlantic, Indian, and Pacific Oceans

Status Not threatened

Dories and Allies

Sticklebacks

The John Dory (*Zeus faber*) is also known as St. Peter's fish. Together with the Cape Dory (*Zeus capensis*) they are the longest of the dories, each growing to a maximum of 36 inches (90 cm).

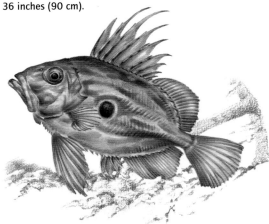

This 4.3-inch (11-cm) male three-spined stickleback (*Gasterosteus aculeatus aculeatus*) constructs a nest from plant material in which the female will lay her eggs. A male's chest turns bright red or orange in the breeding season.

Common name Dories and allies

Families Zeidae (dories), Oreosomatidae (oreos), Caproidae (boarfish)

Order Zeiformes

Number of species Zeidae: 14 in 7 genera; Oreosomatidae: 10 in 4 genera; Caproidae: 12 in 2 genera

Size From around 2.5 in (6.3 cm) to about 36 in (90 cm)

Key features Body highly compressed in all species, very deep in some species; snout pointed to varying degrees; mouth from quite small to extremely large, extendable in all species; large eyes; dorsal fin has spiny front half, soft-rayed back; small strong spines run along both sides of dorsal and anal fins (dories), front dorsal spines very long (John Dory, *Zeus faber*, and others); scales generally small, with sandpaper effect (oreos, boarfish); variable coloration: mottled, silvery-gray to dark, also reds

Breeding Eggs and sperm released into water where they are fertilized; in some species eggs are fertilized inside female, then released; no parental care of eggs or larvae

Diet Fish and invertebrates; also salps (sea squirts)

Habitat Most occur close to seafloor over muddy, sandy, or rocky bottoms, also reefs; a few enter brackish water; all recognized as marine fish; depth from very shallow water, e.g., 16 ft (5 m), to nearly 5,100 ft (1,550 m)

Distribution Antarctic, Atlantic, Indian, and Pacific Oceans, some into major seas like Mediterranean

Status Not threatened

Common name Sticklebacks

Family Gasterosteidae

Order Gasterosteiformes

Number of species 11 in 5 genera

Size From 2 in (5 cm) to 9 in (23 cm)

Key features Elongated, compressed body, with bony plates (scutes) running lengthwise; pointed head; mouth angled upward; eyes relatively large; row of isolated spines running along back and in front of soft dorsal fin; number of spines varies within species, but no spines in Greek nine-spine stickleback (*Pungitius hellenicus*); sometimes pelvic spine and fin lacking; caudal peduncle slim to very slim; coloration: variable, especially in males; blue, green, brown, black, and red (particularly intense during breeding)

Breeding Female lays eggs in nest built by male; young hatch 7–10 days later, protected by male

Diet Invertebrates; also fish eggs, larvae, and small fish

Habitat Pure fresh water through brackish water to fully marine; vegetated areas (preferably with no movement or light currents) and fine-grained bottoms; mostly found in very shallow water, but some occur down to 180 ft (55 m)

Distribution Widely distributed in Northern Hemisphere

Status IUCN lists Greek nine-spine stickleback as Critically Endangered

Sea Horses, Pipefish, and Allies

This 1.2-inch (3-cm) long armored stickleback (*Indostomus paradoxus*) can leap out of the water.

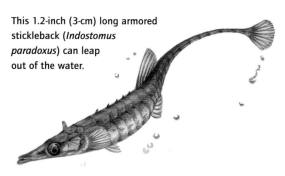

Common name Sea horses, pipefish, and allies

Families Syngnathidae (sea horses, pipefish, pipehorses, seadragons), Solenostomidae (ghost pipefish), Indostomidae (armored sticklebacks)

Subfamilies Syngnathidae: Syngnathinae (pipefish, pipehorses, seadragons); Hippocampinae (sea horses)

Order Gasterosteiformes

Number of species Syngnathidae: around 270 in 52 genera; Solenostomidae: 4 in 1 genus; Indostomidae: 3 in 1 genus

Size From 0.95 in (2.4 cm) to 37.4 in (95 cm)

Key features Elongated body (encased in bony rings or star-shaped plates): held upright (sea horses), or horizontal (pipefish, seadragons); long snout (short in armored sticklebacks), small mouth; 1 to 2 dorsal fins, some with spines and soft rays; some species lack pelvic, caudal, anal fins; long, slim caudal peduncle (armored sticklebacks); varied coloration: muted browns to bright colors; sometimes patterned body or dark bars on fins

Breeding Male carries eggs in belly pouch or mass of spongy tissue (sea horses); female carries eggs in pouch formed by pelvic fin (ghost pipefish)

Diet Invertebrates, worms, and other bottom-dwellers

Habitat Shallow coral reefs, seagrass meadows above 165 ft (50 m) depth or to 310 ft (95 m); some in brackish estuaries; armored sticklebacks in still or slow-moving fresh water, leaf litter on bottom

Distribution Widely distributed in tropical, subtropical, and warm temperate regions of Atlantic, Indian, and Pacific Oceans, and Indo-West Pacific; also Myanmar, Cambodia, Thailand, Mekong Basin

Status IUCN lists 45 sea horse and pipefish species as under threat; sea horse species: 19 Vulnerable, 1 Endangered; pipefish species: 5 Vulnerable, 1 Critically Endangered

Gurnards

The large rays of the pectoral fins of this 35.4-inch (90-cm) flying gurnard (*Dactylopterus volitans*) fan out over the sandy bottom as it searches for its favorite meal of crustaceans, especially crabs, clams, and small fish.

Common name Gurnards

Families Dactylopteridae (flying and helmet gurnards), Triglidae (gurnards and sea robins)

Subfamilies Triglidae: Triglinae (gurnards and sea robins): Peristediinae (armored gurnards and armored sea robins)

Order Scorpaeniformes

Number of species Dactylopteridae: 7 in 2 genera; Triglidae: around 150 in 10 genera

Size From 2.8 in (7cm) to 35.4 in (90 cm)

Key features Elongated body tapering toward tail; scutelike scales (helmet gurnards) or spine-covered plates (armored sea robins); head encased; eye ridges (gurnards), or helmetlike structure (flying and helmet gurnards); mouth located under tip of snout, either blunt (helmet gurnards), or 2 projections (gurnards and sea robins); barbels on underside of lower jaw (armored sea robins); 2 dorsal fins in all species; pectorals large and winglike (helmet gurnards) but smaller in others; several free rays in pectoral fin (gurnards); long spine in pelvic fins (helmet gurnards); varied coloration

Breeding Eggs and sperm released late spring or summer, then abandoned

Diet Bottom-dwelling invertebrates; some fish

Habitat Adults marine, juveniles may enter estuaries; helmet gurnards in tropical waters; mostly sandy bottoms; shallow water less than 655 ft (200 m) deep, some species over 2,950 ft (900 m)

Distribution Dactylopteridae: Atlantic and Indo-Pacific Oceans; Triglidae: most temperate and tropical seas: armored sea robins center on Atlantic, Indian, and Pacific Oceans

Status Not threatened

Sculpins, Poachers, and Allies

Bullheads (*Cottus gobio*) grow up to 7 inches (18 cm). They feed on bottom-dwelling invertebrates, insects, and crustaceans.

Common name Sculpins, poachers, and allies

Families Cottidae (sculpins), Cottocomephridae (Baikal sculpins), Comephoridae (Baikal oilfish), Abyssocottidae (deep-sea sculpins), Rhamphocottidae (grunt sculpin), Ereuniidae (ereunids), Psychrolutidae (fatheads), Agonidae (poachers), Hemitripteridae (hemitripterids), Bathylutichthyidae (bathylutids)

Order Scorpaeniformes

Number of species Cottidae: about 200 to 300 in around 70 genera; Cottocomephridae: 7 in 3 genera; Comephoridae: 2 in 1 genus; Abyssocottidae: about 23 in 6 genera; Rhamphocottidae: 1 in 1 genus; Ereuniidae: 3 in 2 genera; Psychrolutidae: 40 in 10 genera; Agonidae: 46 in about 17 genera; Hemitripteridae: 9 in 3 genera; Bathylutichthyidae: 1 in 1 genus

Size From 0.8 in (2 cm) to 39 in (99 cm)

Key features Slim, elongated bodies (poachers) or robust (fatheads); head long and pointed (poachers), large and less pointed (Baikal oilfish), or blunt (miller's thumb, *Cottus gobio*, and fatheads); mouth often large; usually 2 dorsal fins, anterior spiny and posterior soft-rayed, but only single dorsal fin (some poachers); dorsal, caudal, and anal joined (Bathylutichthyidae); pectoral fins well formed in most species; pectorals have several free rays (Ereuniidae); varied coloration

Breeding Eggs usually laid on roof of cave and guarded by male; most fertilization external

Diet Fish eggs, numerous invertebrates, and other fish

Habitat Fresh waters in streams, rivers, and lakes, to deep polar waters

Distribution Most seas, including polar regions; predominantly Northern Hemisphere

Status IUCN lists 9 species of Cottidae family as: 2 Data Deficient, 4 Vulnerable, 2 Critically Endangered, 1 Extinct

Dottybacks and Allies

All dottybacks and their allies are predatory, but species like the royal gramma (*Gramma loreto*) also feed on the external body parasites of other fish. Length to 3.2 inches (8 cm).

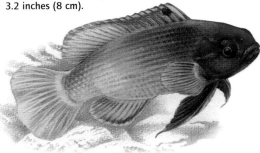

Common name Dottybacks and allies

Families Pseudochromidae (dottybacks), Grammatidae (basslets), Plesiopidae (roundheads), Notograptidae (eel blennies), Opistognathidae (jawfish)

Order Perciformes

Number of species Pseudochromidae: 114 in 17 genera; Grammatidae: about 10 in 2 genera; Plesiopidae: 45 in 11 genera; Notograptidae: 4 in 1 genus; Opistognathidae: 59 in 3 genera

Size From 0.8 in (2 cm) to over 45 in (1.2 m)

Key features Body usually moderately to extremely elongate and eel-like; head usually has relatively large mouth and eyes; mouth bears a central barbel in Notograptidae; dorsal and anal fins long based with spines in front half (*Stalix* species have forked spines in dorsal fin); dorsal, caudal, and anal fins joined in Notograptidae; coloration from drab to bright primary colors

Breeding Generally poorly known; most deposit clumps of eggs on the bottom, which may be defended by the male; some are mouthbrooders; sex changes from female to male occur in some types

Diet Mainly invertebrates

Habitat Mainly shallow or relatively shallow waters, often associated with coral reefs or rubble slopes; few are coastal deepwater species

Distribution All families strictly marine, extending through tropical and subtropical zones of Indo-Pacific, western, and central Atlantic and, in Notograptidae, between southern New Guinea and northern Australia

Status IUCN lists pale dottyback (*Pseudochromis pesi*) as Vulnerable

Remoras and Allies

The sharksucker (*Echeneis naucrates*) is the largest of the remoras, growing to a length of about 43 inches (1.1 m).

Common name Remoras and allies

Families Echeneidae (remoras), Rachycentridae (cobia), Coryphaenidae (dolphinfish)

Order Perciformes

Number of species Echeneidae: 8 in 4 genera; Rachycentridae 1 species; Coryphaenidae 2 in 1 genus

Size From about 12 in (30 cm) to 6.9 ft (2.1 m)

Key features All species elongate; remoras and cobia have flat heads; male dolphinfish have pronounced forehead or crest; eyes large; mouth large; remoras have 2 dorsal fins, the first modified into a sucker; cobia has a long-based, soft dorsal fin preceded by 6–9 isolated short spines; dolphinfish have exceptionally long-based dorsal and anal fins; all other fins well formed, with tail deeply forked in dolphinfish; coloration variable in remoras, ranging from uniform to dark and light longitudinal bands in live sharksucker (*Echeneis naucrates*) and cobia; dolphinfish brilliantly colored in metallic hues

Breeding Eggs scattered in open water and abandoned; larvae of cobia and dolphinfish have spines on their gill covers

Diet All predatory, with remoras feeding mainly on scraps of food from their hosts' meals; cobia and dolphinfish feed on fish, squid, and crustaceans

Habitat All found in open water, with remoras and cobia also in shallower waters in the company of large creatures, including—in the case of remoras—sharks, billfish, and turtles; cobia ranges from the surface down to nearly 4,000 ft (1,200 m); dolphinfish often shelter close to, or beneath, floating objects

Distribution Widespread in Atlantic, Indian, and Pacific Oceans

Status Not threatened

Jacks, Pompanos, and Allies

Occasionally growing up to 4 feet (1.2 m), the crevalle jack (*Caranx hippos*) is a streamlined species often found in shoals around the western Atlantic coast from Novia Scotia to Uruguay. It is fished commercially and for sport, especially around Florida.

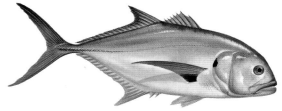

Common name Jacks, pompanos, and allies

Families Carangidae (jacks and pompanos), Menidae (moonfish), Leiognathidae (ponyfish, slimys, or slipmouths), Bramidae (pomfrets)

Order Perciformes

Number of species Carangidae: about 146 in 30 genera; Menidae: 1 species; Leiognathidae: about 39 in 3 genera; Bramidae: 21 in 8 genera

Size From 2 in (5 cm) to 6.5 ft (2 m)

Key features Body shape extremely varied (even within families) from elongated and streamlined to deep bodied, but most species oval shaped; head shape variable from pointed, as in the amberjacks (*Seriola* species), to blunt, as in many pomfrets; bony ridges on top of the head in ponyfish; mouth extendable in ponyfish; eyes moderately large; dorsal fin with long base and spines in front section; anal fin similar but with no spine in the moonfish; tail forked; some species lack pelvic fins; coloration generally drab and dark in many pomfrets to silvery and banded in many jacks and pompanos

Breeding Eggs scattered in open water and abandoned

Diet All predatory; smaller and bottom-dwelling species feed mainly on small invertebrates; large species also eat fish

Habitat Mostly open-water shoaling fish, but some, like the moonfish and the lookdowns (*Selene* species), remain closer to the bottom; all species marine, but some may enter brackish water; some species, notably the pilot fish (*Naucrates ductor*) and the golden trevally (*Gnathanodon speciosus*), accompany large fish such as sharks and manta rays

Distribution Widely distributed in Atlantic, Indian, and Pacific Oceans

Status Not threatened

Porgies and Breams

Archerfish

The common seabream (*Pagrus pagrus*) grows to about 3 feet (91 cm). It is the only member of the family Sparidae under serious threat in the wild, largely due to overfishing.

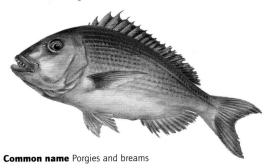

Common name Porgies and breams

Families Sparidae (porgies), Lethrinidae (emperor breams or scavengers), Nemipteridae (threadfin or whiptail breams)

Order Perciformes

Number of species Sparidae: over 120 in 36 genera; Lethrinidae: about 38 in 5 genera; Nemipteridae: about 63 in 5 genera

Size From about 3.7 in (9.5 cm) to 6.6 ft (2 m)

Key features Ranging from extremely elongate, as in bogue (*Boops boops*), to deep, as in longspine porgy (*Stenotomus caprinus*); head usually robust, with snout ranging from pointed, as in black-streaked monocle bream (*Scolopsis taeniatus*), to very blunt, as in musselcracker seabream (*Sparodon durbanensis*); eyes usually large; 1 dorsal fin with spiny front part; anal fin with several spines at front; all fins well formed; variable coloration, often including reflective scales; few species with contrasting coloration, such as black and silver

Breeding Eggs scattered and abandoned; sex changes frequent in all families

Diet Most predatory, taking prey ranging from zooplankton to fish and frequently including crabs, mollusks, and other hard-shelled invertebrates; some species almost exclusively herbivorous, feeding mainly on marine algae

Habitat Most occur at shallow to moderate depths of less than 330 ft (100 m); some range to depths of about 1,310 ft (400 m); habitats vary from sandy to rocky or rubbly, while some are found on coral reefs or seagrass meadows

Distribution Tropical, subtropical, and temperate Atlantic, Indian, and Pacific Oceans

Status IUCN lists common seabream (*Pagrus pagrus*) as Endangered

At 16 to 18 inches (40–45 cm) in length the largescale archerfish (*Toxotes chatareus*) is the largest member of the family Toxotidae.

Common name Archerfish

Family Toxotidae

Order Perciformes

Number of species 6 in 1 genus

Size From about 6 in (15 cm) to 18 in (46 cm)

Key features Body deep and flattened from side to side, although less so in primitive archerfish (*Toxotes lorentzi*); head sharply pointed with flat top; large mouth directed upward at an angle; eyes very large and close to top of head; top of body forms straight line from tip of snout to front of dorsal fin; dorsal and anal fins have a few spines at the front, followed by soft, branched rays; tail, pectoral, and pelvic fins well formed; all species except primitive archerfish basically silver bodied with dark bands or blotches along top half; primitive archerfish lacks the bold black blotches; dorsal and anal fins may be dusky with some yellow, particularly in smallscale archerfish (*T. microlepis*)

Breeding Very few details available, but largescale archerfish (*T. chatareus*) reported to lay between 20,000 and 150,000 eggs, in either fresh or brackish water

Diet Mainly insects and other invertebrates, frequently, but not always, knocked off foliage with water drops; also smaller fish; largescale and common archerfish (*T. jaculatrix*) eat some plant matter

Habitat Predominantly marine, but all species spend periods in fresh water, especially the smallscale, primitive, and western archerfish (*T. oligolepis*)—these species frequently found in swamps and streams, often with overhanging vegetation; common and largescale archerfish typically found in brackish mangrove swamps and estuaries

Distribution From India to the Philippines, Australia, and Polynesia

Status Not threatened

Butterflyfish

The 8-inch (20-cm) copperband or beaked butterflyfish (*Chelmon rostratus*) is found in the Indian and Pacific Oceans.

Common name Butterflyfish

Family Chaetodontidae

Order Perciformes

Number of species About 128 in 11 genera

Size From 3 in (7.6 cm) to 12 in (30 cm); most species 4.7–10 in (12–25 cm)

Key features Body flattened from side to side and usually quite deep; head pointed, particularly in species that extract food from crevices or polyps; small mouth at tip of snout; dorsal fin with spiny front section and soft-rayed back; anal fin with 3–5 spines at front; all fins well formed; body scales extend onto both dorsal and anal fins; most species brightly colored, often with vertical bands; eye frequently hidden by a vertical band or patch; false eyes or eye-spots common on either body or back lower edge of the dorsal fin; many species develop night colors that differ from the day ones; colors of juveniles frequently different

Breeding Eggs released into water and unprotected; hatch in 18–30 hours; larvae have distinctive bony plates during free-swimming planktonic stage, which may last from a few weeks to several months

Diet Most feed on small invertebrates, coral polyps or tentacles, zooplankton, algae, or fish eggs; some species very specialized feeders

Habitat Mainly found in water less than 65 ft (20 m) deep, mostly on coral reefs; some species in rubble zones and water down to 656 ft (200 m)

Distribution Tropical and subtropical Indo-Pacific plus warm-temperate Atlantic

Status IUCN lists 5 *Chaetodon* species as Vulnerable

Angelfish

The regal angelfish (*Pygoplites diacanthus*) of the Indo-Pacific grows to about 10 inches (25 cm) in length. Often found near caves, it feeds on sponges and other small invertebrates. It may appear in shoals or solitarily.

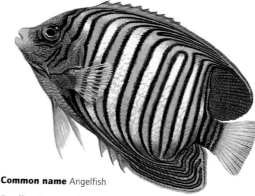

Common name Angelfish

Family Pomacanthidae

Order Perciformes

Number of species About 85 in 7 genera

Size From 2.4 in (6 cm) to 24 in (60 cm)

Key features Body strongly flattened from side to side and usually quite deep; head blunt to slightly pointed; small mouth located at tip of snout; bone in front of gill cover carries a stout spine; dorsal fin has spiny front section and soft-rayed back section; anal fin has 3 spines at the front and soft-rayed back section; all other fins well formed; striking coloration in many species, particularly in pygmy angels; juveniles often have completely different coloration and patterning than adults

Breeding Eggs released into water while spawning above the reef and then abandoned; hatching may take 18–30 hours; larvae have spiny scales (but not bony plates) and are planktonic for a while

Diet *Centropyge* species feed mainly on algae; *Genicanthus* species prefer zooplankton; most other species feed on sea squirts, sponges, soft corals, sea pens, other invertebrates, and algae

Habitat Most species found on shallow-water tropical reefs; a few, such as the masked angelfish (*G. personatus*), are found in deeper water; angelfish are very rarely found in open sandy areas

Distribution Widely distributed in all tropical seas, with nearly 90 percent of species in Indo-Pacific

Status IUCN lists resplendent angelfish (*C. resplendens*) as Vulnerable

Chameleon Fish and Leaffish

The Amazon leaffish (*Monocirrhus polyacanthus*) is an efficient predator that uses its leaflike appearance to drift close to unsuspecting prey. Length to 3.2 inches (8 cm).

Common name Chameleon fish, leaffish, and pikehead

Families Badidae, Nandidae, Luciocephalidae

Order Perciformes

Number of species Badidae (chameleon fish): 15 in 2 genera; Nandidae (leaffish): about 8 in 4 genera; Luciocephalidae (pikehead): 1 species

Size From about 1.9 in (4.8 cm) to 8.3 in (21 cm)

Key features Body elongate in chameleon fish, deeper and more compressed in leaffish; mouth large to very large in most species except chameleon fish; head pointed; eyes medium to large; dorsal fin has long base occupying most of back, with front half armed with spines; rounded tail; lateral line incomplete or missing; coloration: most leaffish mottled shades of brown and tan; chameleon fish extremely variable, with colorful fins, body spots, and patches that change rapidly according to mood

Breeding Common chameleon fish (*Badis badis*) lays up to 100 eggs in a cave where male guards them until they hatch after about 3 days; Amazon leaffish (*Monocirrhus polyacanthus*) and Guyana leaffish (*Polycentrus schomburgkii*) lay up to 300 or 600 eggs respectively on a leaf, and male guards them for about 4 days until they hatch; eggs of *Nandus* species (and probably others) scattered and abandoned

Diet Ranges from small invertebrates to sizable fish

Habitat Common, Bornean (*N. nebulosus*), and Guyana leaffish occur in fresh and brackish water; other species exclusively in fresh water, in wide range of habitats from ditches and swamps to streams, rivers, and pools

Distribution Amazon and Guyana leaffish: northeastern South America; *Afronandus* and *Polycentropsis* spp: tropical West Africa; *Nandus* spp: Pakistan to Borneo; chameleon fish widely distributed in Pakistan and Burma

Status Not threatened

Gouramis

The 2.5 inch (6.5-cm) Siamese fighting fish (*Betta splendens*) is a popular aquarium fish. It is famed not only for the aggressive disputes between males but also for its bubble-nest building and the magnificent fins of cultured varieties.

Common name Gouramis

Families Helostomatidae, Osphronemidae, Belontiidae

Order Perciformes

Number of species About 90 in 14–15 genera

Size From about 1 in (2.5 cm) to 30 in (76 cm)

Key features Body ranges from slim-bodied, pointed-snout species such as licorice (*Parosphromenus* spp.) and croaking gouramis (*Trichopsis* spp.) to oval-shaped, round-snouted species such as giant gourami (*Osphronemus* spp.); teeth lacking in jawbones of some species; eyes usually relatively large; most species have filamentlike elongations on pelvic fins, most pronounced in *Osphronemus*, *Colisa*, and *Trichogaster* spp. but totally lacking in kissing gourami (*Helostoma temminckii*); dorsal fin narrow based in fighters, croakers, *Trichogaster* spp, and pointed-tail gourami (*Malpulatta kretseri*); considerably wider in others, particularly *Colisa* spp. and kissing gourami; tail ranges from pointed to almost straight; coloration very variable, more pronounced in males than females

Breeding Bubble-nesting species build nests on water surface or under overhang or submerged leaf; mouthbrooding species incubate eggs inside mouth of one parent

Diet Plants and animals, particularly small invertebrates

Habitat Wide range of still waters, often with overhanging and submerged vegetation; includes waters that may become depleted of oxygen for part of year; some species, e.g., pointed-tail gourami, found in secluded flowing waters

Distribution Widely distributed in Southeast Asia, India, Pakistan, Thailand, and Malay Archipelago

Status IUCN lists 14 species as under threat

Cichlids

The blue-white labido (*Labidochromis caeruleus*) comes from the northwestern coast of Africa's Lake Malawi. The eggs are brooded in the females' mouths, and the fry also retreat there at any sign of danger. Length to 3.2 inches (8 cm).

Common name Cichlids

Family Cichlidae

Order Perciformes

Number of species Probably over 2,000 in over 105 genera

Size From 1.5 in (3.5 cm) to about 36 in (90 cm)

Key features Mostly oval but ranging from almost circular in discus (*Symphysodon* spp.) to slim and elongate in pike cichlids (*Crenicichla* spp.); head rounded to pointed, with small lips or large fleshy ones; teeth usually brown-tipped but vary in shape according to diet; eyes usually quite large; front half of dorsal fin has hard, unbranched spines, back half has soft, branched rays; anal fin similar but with shorter base; caudal fin well formed; coloration very variable—males usually more colorful

Breeding Adults typically protect eggs and young; some are substrate spawners, laying eggs on specially prepared sites such as rocks, leaves, or snail shells; some are mouthbrooders—males attract females to the spawning sites, and females incubate the eggs in their mouths

Diet Most eat a wide range of animals, although many also eat plants; specialized feeders graze on algae and microorganisms, some on scales or eyes of other fish

Habitat From shallow, shaded forest streams and deep, wide rivers to estuaries, marshes, lakes, and backwaters; most occur in fresh water

Distribution Central and South America, southern U.S., West Indies, African rift lakes (Malawi, Tanganyika, Victoria, and others), tropical Africa, India, Sri Lanka, Syria, Israel, Iran, Madagascar

Status IUCN lists 154 species as under various levels of threat

Wrasses

The clown coris (*Coris aygula*) feeds mainly on hard-shelled invertebrates such as mollusks and sea urchins. It is sometimes caught commercially and as a game fish. The specimen shown here is a juvenile, complete with false eyes on its fins. Length to 4 feet (1.2 m).

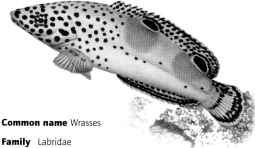

Common name Wrasses

Family Labridae

Order Perciformes

Number of species 450–500 in more than 60 genera

Size From about 1.8 in (4.5 cm) to over 8 ft (2.5 m); majority of species 6–8 in (15–20 cm)

Key features Mostly relatively elongated, with some, such as cleaner wrasses, slim and almost cylindrical in cross-section; many larger species deeper-bodied; head usually pointed; extendable jaw; forward-pointing front teeth, usually with gap between; all fins well formed; front part of dorsal and anal fin have hard, unjointed spines (more in dorsal than anal), followed by soft, branched rays; body scales cycloid; coloration very diverse and usually much more intense in males than females

Breeding Spawning occurs in pairs or shoals; males and females swim together from the reef toward surface, releasing eggs and sperm into water; eggs float to the surface, where they hatch

Diet Predatory; smaller species feed primarily on invertebrates; larger species also feed on other fish; specialized feeders include cleaner wrasses that feed on external parasites of other fish; some larger wrasses feed on toxic organisms such as seastars, urchins, boxfish, and seahares

Habitat Tropical, temperate, and subarctic coastal waters, preferring rocky and reef habitats

Distribution Widely distributed in the Atlantic, Indian, and Pacific Oceans and most seas, including the Mediterranean and Red Sea

Status IUCN lists 6 species as under various levels of threat, including the giant wrasse (*Cheilinus undulatus*) as Endangered

Parrotfish

The rusty parrotfish (*Scarus ferrugineus*) is found on reefs from about 3 feet (1 m) down to about 200 feet (60 m) in the western Indian Ocean. Length to 16 inches (41 cm).

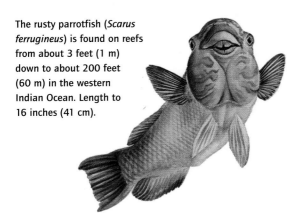

Common name Parrotfish

Family Scaridae

Order Perciformes

Number of species About 94 species in 10 genera

Size From about 5 in (13 cm) to about 51 in (1.3 m); most species are 12–20 in (30–50 cm)

Key features Body often elongated oval shape; some of smallest species somewhat slimmer, while green humphead (*Bolbometopon muricatum*) is deeper just behind head; head usually tapers to rounded snout, but green humphead has high, bulbous forehead; teeth fused to form prominent parrotlike beak; all fins well formed; dorsal and anal fins have hard, unbranched, pointed spines at the front (many more in dorsal than anal), followed by soft, branched rays; pelvic fin has prominent spine at front; caudal fin may have extended top and bottom rays; body scales usually large and cycloid

Breeding Most individuals change sex as they mature; in initial mature phase most are drab breeding females with a few drab primary males; in next (terminal) phase females become brightly colored secondary males, some of which become dominant, although some primary males will mate

Diet Most species herbivorous; most also take in coral fragments that are ground up in the gut to crush algal cells and make them digestible; a few species are live coral eaters

Habitat Most species found on coral reefs; a few may occur in seagrass meadows and on rocky reefs

Distribution Mostly tropical Atlantic, Indian, and Pacific Oceans, Red Sea, Caribbean, plus a few species in Mediterranean

Status IUCN lists rainbow parrotfish (*Scarus guacamaia*) as Vulnerable

Gobies

The 4.5-inch (11-cm) sand goby (*Pomatoschistus minutus*) lives in temperate brackish or marine waters, where it feeds mainly on marine worms and crustaceans.

Common name Gobies

Families Gobiidae (gobies), Eleotridae (sleeper gobies, sleepers, or gudgeons), Rhyacichthyidae (loach gobies)

Order Perciformes

Number of species Gobiidae: 2,000 in about 212 genera; Eleotridae: about 150 in 35 genera; Rhyacichthyidae: about 92 in about 21 genera

Size From 0.3 in (7.6 mm) to about 28 in (71 cm); most species are between 3–8 in (7.5–20 cm)

Key features Body elongate and often almost cylindrical in cross-section; mouth usually large, often with fleshy lips; eyes near top of head; first dorsal fin with hard, unbranched spines and second with soft, branched rays; pelvic fins may form sucker (gobies) or range from free to almost fused (sleepers); tail usually rounded; coloration variable—many bottom-living species cryptically mottled, others brilliantly colored, with first dorsal fin frequently colorful in males

Breeding Eggs usually laid on precleaned site such as a rock or roof of a cave and guarded by male

Diet Most feed on invertebrates; midwater species usually feed on plankton; larger species may also eat smaller fish

Habitat Most occur either in brackish or marine conditions; some occur in fresh water; many can tolerate wide salinity range; exceptional habitats include fast-flowing mountain streams, caves, and tidal mudflats; some form associations with totally unrelated creatures like sea urchins and shrimp

Distribution Mainly in tropical and temperate regions; only a few species found in cooler waters

Status IUCN lists 58 gobies and 4 sleeper gobies as threatened; 5 are Critically Endangered, including Elizabeth Springs goby (*Chlamydogobius micropterus*) and dwarf pygmy goby (*Pandaka pygmaea*); 17 species are listed as Vulnerable

Barracudas

At 12 inches (30 cm) in length the yellowstripe barracuda (*Sphyraena chrysotaenia*) of the Indo-Pacific and Mediterranean is a relatively small species.

Common name Barracudas

Family Sphyraenidae

Order Perciformes

Number of species 25 in 1 genus (*Sphryraena*)

Size From about 12 in (30 cm) to 6.7 ft (2.1 m); at least half of all species grow to over 39 in (1 m)

Key features All species elongated with pointed head and forked tail; mouth large with numerous, powerful fanglike teeth; lower jaw slightly longer than upper jaw; large eyes; two widely separated dorsal fins; most fins except tail relatively small; lateral line well developed; coloration usually includes dark blue on back, shading to silvery along the belly; body often attractively marked with vertical bands; fins may be colored

Breeding Spawning usually occurs in groups in open water; eggs scattered and abandoned; few other details known

Diet Almost exclusively fish, including smaller barracuda and squid; many smaller species also regularly eat shrimp

Habitat Frequently found near the surface but may descend to depths of about 330 ft (100 m); may be found close to shore, in harbors and lagoons, or in open seas; young may enter brackish water around estuaries and mangroves

Distribution Widespread in tropical and subtropical Atlantic, Indian, and Pacific Oceans

Status Not threatened

Mackerels and Tunas

The Atlantic mackerel (*Scomber scombrus*) is one of the world's most important commercial fish species. Many thousands of tons are caught each year. Length to 24 inches (60 cm).

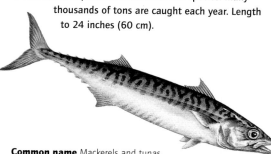

Common name Mackerels and tunas

Family Scombridae

Order Perciformes

Number of species About 54 species in 15 genera

Size From about 8 in (20 cm) to 15 ft (4.6 m)

Key features Body spindle shaped and almost cylindrical in cross-section; head pointed; large eyes halfway between back of upper jaw and top of head; first dorsal fin with hard spines; both fins fit into grooves when folded back; pectoral fins with hard leading edge; finlets behind 2nd dorsal and anal fins extend to base of tail; tail lunate with hard, stiff leading edge; 2 keels on either side of caudal peduncle; scales very small; most species have blue backs and silvery bellies; bonitos usually have longitudinal stripes on body; mackerels usually have spots or dark streaks on upper half of body

Breeding All are egg scatterers; a northern bluefin tuna (*Thunnus thynnus*) weighing 600–660 lb (270–300 kg) can produce 10 million eggs in a single spawning; skipjack tuna (*Katsuwonus pelamis*) may breed all year in tropics; others such as northern bluefin have narrow spawning seasons; southern bluefin tuna (*T. maccoyii*) may spawn only once in a lifetime; hatching may take as little as 3 days

Diet Mostly smaller fish, squid, and crustaceans; some smaller species also sift zooplankton

Habitat Open water, frequently near surface but some down to about 820 ft (250 m); a few, notably the albacore (*T. alalunga*), may descend to about 1,970 ft (600 m)

Distribution Widely distributed in tropical and subtropical seas; some species are restricted, such as the Monterey Spanish mackerel (*Scomberomorus concolor*), which is endemic to the northern part of the Gulf of California

Status IUCN lists 5 species as under various levels of threat, including southern bluefin tuna as Critically Endangered

Swordfish and Marlins

At about a maximum length of 16.4 feet (5 m) the Atlantic blue marlin (*Makaira nigricans*) is one of the largest and most impressive of the billfish. It ranges through temperate and tropical seas worldwide, usually in open waters.

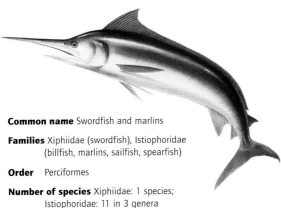

Common name Swordfish and marlins

Families Xiphiidae (swordfish), Istiophoridae (billfish, marlins, sailfish, spearfish)

Order Perciformes

Number of species Xiphiidae: 1 species; Istiophoridae: 11 in 3 genera

Size From about 6 ft (1.8 m) to 16.4 ft (5 m)

Key features All species elongate with a sword or bill: shortest in shortbill spearfish (*Tetrapturus angustirostris*); in swordfish (*Xiphias gladius*) sword is flattened from top to bottom and has sharp edges; in all other species sword is round in cross-section; body almost cylindrical in cross-section; eyes well formed; swordfish lack jaw teeth; dorsal fin narrow based in swordfish and long based in others; sail-like in sailfish (*Istiophorus* spp.); pelvic fins absent in swordfish, narrow but present in others; caudal peduncle has 1 keel on either side in swordfish and 2 keels in others; tail stiff, narrow, and well forked; coloration blackish fading to light brown or gray in swordfish; blue-black on back, shading to silvery flanks in marlins (*Makaira* spp.) and relatives; some species have vertical blue stripes

Breeding Generally occurs in relatively shallow water; single female may be courted by 1 or more males; millions of eggs produced in a single spawning

Diet Mainly fish, squid, and crustaceans

Habitat Open waters, including midocean; some species also frequent coastal waters; most remain in warmer surface waters above the thermocline

Distribution Most tropical and subtropical waters

Status IUCN lists swordfish as Data Deficient

Flounders

The bony ridge of this 40-inch (1-m) European plaice (*Pleuronectes platessa*) is visible behind its eyes. Lying flat on the rocky bottom of very shallow brackish or marine waters, it hunts for its favorite mollusks at night.

Common name Flounders

Families Bothidae (lefteye flounders), Pleuronectidae (righteye flounders)

Order Pleuronectiformes

Number of species Bothidae: about 157 in 20 genera; Pleuronectidae: nearly 120 in about 44 genera

Size From 1.4 in (3.5 cm) to 8.5 ft (2.6 m)

Key features Asymmetrical, oval-shaped bodies; head with both eyes on same (top) side; front edge of dorsal fin located above or in front of eyes; all fins separate from each other; pelvic fins asymmetrical in lefteyes, symmetrical in righteyes; coloration: top side heavily patterned in many species; capable of rapid color changes

Breeding About 2 million eggs released

Diet Invertebrates; larger species also take fish

Habitat Nearly always marine; Bothidae: tropical and temperate zones; usually over fine-grained bottoms; shallow or relatively shallow waters, normally above 330 ft (100 m); Pleuronectidae: tropical, subtropical, temperate, and (almost) Arctic zones; usually over fine-grained bottoms; depths above 660 ft (200 m); some species may enter brackish water

Distribution Atlantic, Indian, and Pacific Oceans; Pleuronectidae: also Arctic Ocean

Status IUCN lists Atlantic halibut (*Hippoglossus hippoglossus*) as Endangered and yellowtail flounder (*Limanda ferriginea*) as Vulnerable

Triggerfish and Filefish

The 12-inch (30-cm) Picasso triggerfish (*Rhinecanthus aculeatus*) is commonly found in subtidal reef flats and shallow protected lagoons in the Indo-Pacific from the Red Sea down to South Africa and east to Hawaii.

Common name Triggerfish and filefish

Families Balistidae (triggerfish), Monacanthidae (filefish or leatherjackets)

Order Tetraodontiformes

Number of species Balistidae: 40 in about 11 genera; Monacanthidae: 104 in about 31 genera

Size From 1 in (2.5 cm) to 43.3 in (110 cm)

Key features Body usually compressed, roughly oval in shape; triggerfish body less deep, filefish covered in scales with several small spines on outer edge; mouth at tip of snout armed with powerful teeth; eyes set well back on head and toward top; 3 spines (2 in filefish) on first dorsal fin, last is very small; soft rays on second dorsal; well-formed caudal, often with extensions of topmost and lowermost rays; anal almost identical to second dorsal; pelvic fin has 1 spine and attached fold of skin; varied coloration: often spectacular, but sometimes unicolor in triggerfish

Breeding Eggs laid on site prepared by male; female triggerfish guard eggs, but males in filefish; some subtropical filefish release eggs in open water

Diet Sea urchins; also crustaceans (e.g., crabs), hard-shelled mollusks (e.g., snails), algae, worms, eggs, sea squirts, corals, zooplankton; also bottom-dwelling invertebrates

Habitat Most species tropical or subtropical, but some extend into more temperate areas; frequently associated with coral reefs and shallow water, usually less than 165 ft (50 m) deep; some filefish prefer sandy or other fine-grained bottoms or seagrass meadows

Distribution Atlantic, Indian, and Pacific Oceans

Status IUCN lists Queen triggerfish (*Balistes vetula*) as Vulnerable

Boxfish and Cowfish

The 18-inch (46-cm) longhorn cowfish (*Lactoria cornuta*) is found in the Red Sea east to Polynesia and north to Japan. It inhabits weedy areas near rocks or reefs at depths of between 60 and 330 feet (18–100 m).

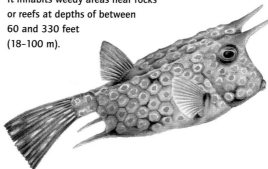

Common name Boxfish and cowfish

Family Ostraciidae (sometimes called Ostraciontidae)

Order Tetraodontiformes

Number of species 37 in 12 genera

Size 4.3 in (11 cm) to 21.7 in (55 cm)

Key features Body cubical or slightly longer and angular, encased in bony carapace or "shell" covered in thin, fleshy tissue; mouth small and partly beaklike; forehead may have hornlike projections; eyes located high on head; single dorsal fin placed well back on body, lacks hard spines; no pelvic skeleton or pelvic fins; coloration extremely variable and often bright: ranging from almost yellow all over to green with blue spots to deep-based colors highlighted with light spots

Breeding Most species have harem system of single male and several females; eggs released into water (often at dusk) and abandoned; hatching takes about 2 days

Diet Bottom-living invertebrates; also seagrasses

Habitat Mainly shallow-water reefs; some species found in seagrass meadows or sand, rocks, or rubble; members of subfamily Aracaninae prefer deeper waters down to 660 ft (200 m)

Distribution Tropical, subtropical, and sometimes temperate regions of Atlantic, Indian, and Pacific Oceans

Status Not threatened

Puffers and Porcupinefish

Molas

This 4.3-inch (11-cm) Valentinni's sharpnose puffer (*Canthigaster valentini*) lives among coral in lagoons and reefs.

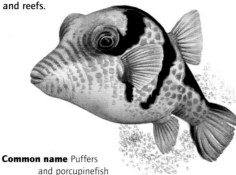

Common name Puffers and porcupinefish

Families Triodontidae (three-toothed puffer or pursefish), Tetraodontidae (puffers), Diodontidae (porcupinefish or burrfish)

Order Tetraodontiformes

Number of species Triodontidae: 1 in 1 genus; Tetraodontidae: 176 in 27 genera; Diodontidae: 20 in 7 genera

Size From 1.6 in (4 cm) to 48 in (1.2 m)

Key features Body elongated, almost spherical if inflated; roundly pointed snout, mouth at tip; fused jaw teeth project into beaklike structure: 2 fused teeth (porcupinefish), 3 (three-toothed puffer), 4 (other puffers); eyes high on head; body scaleless or short, pricklelike scales along belly (puffers), sharp spines (porcupinefish); belly with large purselike sac (three-toothed puffer); dorsal and anal fins set well back on body; no pelvic fins; coloration: variable, often brilliant, with spots and patches (puffers); belly "purse" has yellow ring circling prominent black "eye spot"; darker and lighter shades of brown (porcupinefish)

Breeding Spawn in groups in shallow nests in shallow beach areas after new and full moon; freshwater species spawn in pairs, male guards eggs or fry; eggs hatch in under 2 days or up to a month depending on species; planktonic larvae

Diet Invertebrates including sea urchins and starfish; also other fish and plants ·

Habitat Mostly marine: tropical or subtropical; or fresh brackish water; fine-grained to rocky bottoms; shallow water down to 1,000 ft (300 m)

Distribution Atlantic, Indian, and Pacific Oceans

Status IUCN lists 2 species as Vulnerable

The 11-foot (3.3-m) ocean sunfish (*Mola mola*) drifts at the surface while lying on its side or swims upright with its dorsal fin projecting above the water. It is believed the mola is the heaviest bony fish, up to 5,070 lb (2,300 kg), and produces the most eggs (300 million).

Common names Molas

Family Molidae

Order Tetraodontiformes

Number of species 4 in 3 genera

Size 40 in (1 m) to 11 ft (3.3 m)

Key features Scaleless body relatively compressed (i.e., flattened side to side), almost circular, but slightly elongated in some species; head rounded; small mouth with 2 fused jaw teeth; tiny nostrils on each side of head; eyes small; gill slits are small openings at base of pectoral fins; no pelvic fins or true caudal fin; dorsal and anal fins long and spineless; pseudo-tail formed from last rays of dorsal and anal fins; coloration: drab bluish-brown on back, fading to lighter shades down sides and along belly; brighter in some species

Breeding Vast numbers of small eggs produced, especially by large female ocean sunfish (*Mola mola)*, which can produce 300 million or more; eggs and sperm scattered in open water, then abandoned; larvae with body spines that initially increase in number and are later absorbed

Diet Mainly jellyfish and other soft-bodied invertebrates; also crustaceans, sea urchins, fish, and seaweed

Habitat Open sea, usually close to surface; some species dive deeper, from 900 ft (300 m) down to 2,200 ft (760 m)

Distribution Tropical, subtropical, and warm temperate regions worldwide

Status Not threatened

Glossary

Words in SMALL CAPITALS refer to other entries in the glossary.

Adipose fin fatty fin located behind rayed DORSAL FIN in some fish

Anal fin fin located near the anus

Barbel whiskerlike, sensory growth on the jaws of some fish

Cartilaginous formed of cartilage

Caudal fin "tail" fin

Caudal peduncle part of the body where the tail begins

CITES Convention on International Trade in Endangered Species; an agreement between nations restricting international trade

Countershading color distribution seen in many fish in which the back is darker than the belly

Ctenoid scale similar to the CYCLOID SCALE but with a toothed rear edge

Cycloid scale thin, flexible overlapping scale found in modern bony fish; the front edge of each scale is embedded in a special pouch in the surface of the skin; the back edge is free and smooth or wavy (crenulated) but not toothed

Demersal living near, deposited on, or sinking to the bottom of the sea

Dorsal relating to the upper surface

Dorsal fin(s) fin(s) on a fish's back

Fry young fish

Genus (pl. genera) group of closely related SPECIES

Gill organ by which a fish absorbs dissolved oxygen from the water and gets rid of carbon dioxide

Gill slit slit between the GILLS that allows water to pass through

Gonopodium modified ANAL FIN found in male LIVEBEARERS; used to inseminate females

Hermaphrodite organism with both male and female reproductive organs

Heterocercal term used to describe a tail (CAUDAL FIN) in which the upper LOBE contains the tip of the backbone; in such fins the upper lobe is usually much larger than the lower lobe

IUCN the International Union for the Conservation of Nature assigns plants and animals to internationally agreed categories of rarity. (*See* table below.)

Lateral line organ series of small fluid-filled pits linked to tubes that are connected to a common canal; detects vibrations in the water

Livebearer SPECIES in which males introduce sperm directly into the female's body, resulting in internal fertilization; female generally retains developing embryos until birth

Lobe a rounded projection or division of a bodily part or organ

Median fins fins located on lengthwise middle line of the body, e.g., DORSAL, CAUDAL, or ANAL fins

Metamorphosis changes undergone by an animal as it develops from the embryonic to the adult stage

Operculum bone forming the GILL cover in fish

Orbital relating to the eyes

Papilla (pl. papillae) small, usually cone-shaped projection

Pectoral fin one of the paired FINS connected to the pectoral girdle

Plankton the generally minute animals and plants that drift in marine and fresh water

Proboscis elongated trunklike snout or projection

Ray small spine that acts as a support for the fin membrane

Rostral associated with a rostrum (meaning snout)

Scute platelike, modified scale

Species a population or series of populations that interbreed freely but do not breed with other species

Spiracle porelike opening associated with the GILLS

Swim bladder gas-filled sac in the body cavity of most bony fish; the amount of gas can be regulated, allowing the fish to rise or sink

Ventral relating to the underside

Viviparous producing live offspring

Further Reading

Allen, T. B., *Shark Attacks: their Causes and Avoidance*, The Lyons Press, New York, NY, 2001.

Allen, T. B., *The Shark Almanac*, The Lyons Press, New York, NY, 2003.

Campbell, A., and J. Dawes, (eds.), *The New Encyclopedia of Aquatic Life*, Facts On File, New York, NY, 2004.

Dawes, J., *Complete Encyclopedia of the Freshwater Aquarium*, Firefly Books, Richmond Hill, Canada, 2001.

Gilbert, C. R., and J. D. Williams, *National Audubon Society Field Guide to Fishes*, Alfred A. Knopf, New York, NY, 2002.

Kobayagawa, M., and W. E. Burgess (eds.), *The World of Catfishes*, T. F. H. Publications, Neptune City, NJ, 1991.

Meinkoth, N. A., *National Audubon Society Field Guide to North American Seashore Creatures*, Alfred A. Knopf, New York, NY, 1998.

Nelson, J. S., *Fishes of the World* (3rd edn.), John Wiley & Sons, New York, NY, 1994.

Page, L. M., and B. M. Burr, *A Field Guide to Freshwater Fishes (North America, North of Mexico)* (Peterson Field Guide Series), Houghton Mifflin, Boston, MA, 1991.

Quinn, J. R., *Piranhas: Fact and Fiction*, T. F. H. Publications, Neptune City, NJ, 1992.

Reebs, S. *Fish Behavior in the Aquarium and in the Wild*, Cornell University Press, Ithaca, NY, 2001.

Useful Web Sites

http://www.asmfc.org/speciesDocuments/eel/eelProfile.pdf
Detailed information about the American eel.

http://www.fishbase.org/home.htm
An interesting Web site full of information even on obscure fish, with references to other sources.

http://www.si.edu/resource/faq/nmnh/fish.htm
A useful list of alternative reference for all kinds of fish.

http://www.elasmo-research.org/education/education.htm
The ReefQuest Centre for Shark Research. A very informative site covering all types of sharks and rays.

IUCN CATEGORIES

EX Extinct, when there is no reasonable doubt that the last individual of the species has died.

EW Extinct in the Wild, when a species is known only to survive in captivity or as a naturalized population well outside the past range.

CR Critically Endangered, when a species is facing an extremely high risk of extinction in the wild in the immediate future.

EN Endangered, when a species is facing a very high risk of extinction in the wild in the near future.

VU Vulnerable, when a species is facing a high risk of extinction in the wild in the medium-term future.

LR Lower Risk, when a species has been evaluated and does not satisfy the criteria for CR, EN, or VU.

DD Data Deficient, when there is not enough information about a species to assess the risk of extinction.

NE Not Evaluated, species that have not been assessed by the IUCN criteria.

Index